Li

COUNTRIES, C... ...RIES
Loose Wolf EDUCATION

...ed on or

Also by the Loose Women

Loose Women: Girls' Night In
Loose Women: Here Come the Girls
The Little Book of Loose Women

loosewomen

Loose Women On Men

HODDER

First published in Great Britain in 2010 by Hodder & Stoughton
An Hachette UK company

First published in paperback in 2011

1

Loose Women is an ITV Studios Ltd Production
Copyright © ITV Studios Ltd 2010
Licensed by ITV Global Entertainment

The right of *Loose Women* to be identified as the Author of the Work has been
asserted by them in accordance with the Copyright, Designs and Patents Act 1988.

A CIP catalogue record for this title is available from the British Library.

ISBN 978 1 444 70021 3

Typeset in Adobe Caslon by Hewer Text UK Ltd, Edinburgh

Printed and bound by Clays Ltd, St Ives plc

Hodder & Stoughton policy is to use papers that are natural, renewable and recyclable
products and made from wood grown in sustainable forests. The logging and manufacturing
processes are expected to conform to the environmental regulations of the country of origin.

Hodder & Stoughton Ltd
338 Euston Road
London NW1 3BH

www.hodder.co.uk

To Loose Women Everywhere

Acknowledgements

Following the success of our first three books *Girls' Night In*, *Here Come the Girls!* and *The Little Book of Loose Women*, we were delighted to have the opportunity to write a book about our favourite subject – men! As always our talented writer Rebecca Cripps deserves a big thank you for bringing all our stories and experiences together!

We would also like to thank the *Loose Women* production team who have worked on *Loose Women on Men*; in particular Fiona Keenaghan, Karl Newton, Donna Gower, Emily Humphries, Kevin Morgan, Sarfaraz Hussain and Niall Flanagan.

Last but not least, every good book needs a great publisher and we have been very lucky once again to have had the incredible support and talents of Hodder & Stoughton, in particular our editor Fenella Bates and her team Ciara Foley, Susan Spratt, Sarah Christie and Emma Knight.

CONTENTS

Acknowledgements   **vii**

Introduction   **1**

1. First impressions   **10**
2. Getting to know you . . .   **36**
3. Image and sexuality   **90**
4. Men: the inside story   **132**
5. In the family way   **194**
6. Bits and pieces   **268**

Conclusion   **292**

Introduction

Love 'em, hate 'em, can't live *with* or without them; just where would we be if it weren't for the men in our lives? OK, they drive us up the wall from time to time. Their socks smell; they have strange fixations with things like golf and power drills; and they can be as romantic as porridge. But they also set off butterfly wings in our hearts, ignite our feverish passion and even transport us back into love's young dream every now and then. Plus, without them, we'd barely have anything to talk about! Or moan about!

With two number one titles under our belts, we've gone and devoted a whole book to our favourite subject: men and all their foibles! Yes, ladies, this is the one you've been waiting for, the sauciest, most provocative and fascinating guide to the male species that you're ever likely to read. It may be cold outside, but it's sizzling hot in here: these red-hot pages are packed with startling new revelations, hilarious insights and electrifying confessions. This book is full of brand new material on the topic we spend most of our time thinking about – and we've probably devoted far too much of it to sex! Oh, we just can't help ourselves . . .

Is it possible to understand men completely? Are they cavemen deep down, knights in shining armour, or both? Do they care about our cellulite, or whether we earn more than they do? From the thrills of teenage lust to the perils of midlife crisis, from one-night stands to long-term relationships, from seduction to snoring: we've got it covered!

We're not exactly experts, or even sexperts – although some of us think we are! But we are women who have really lived and experienced more than our fair share of love, passion, drama and heartbreak. So there's lots in here about all the men we've known, from thoughtful reflection on the influence of our dads and granddads, to side-splitting commentary on the impact of first crushes, disastrous dates and dastardly exes. Who hasn't had to kiss a few frogs, eh? We all have! Some of us even married one – or two!

So are you ready to dig deep into the male psyche? Be warned: it's scorching stuff, so best keep your oven gloves at the ready in case it gets too hot to handle!

About Us . . .

COLEEN NOLAN

Although Coleen has been with hubby Ray Fensome for ten years now, he never ceases to surprise her. Yet it was Coleen who made the first move on Ray a decade ago; she knew he was the one from day two, so what was the point in hanging around? He may not always be as romantic as she would like him to be, but he's absolutely brilliant at sewing!

The youngest of eight children, Coleen is a member of the internationally famous pop group The Nolan Sisters. She is also the author of three bestsellers herself, including her debut novel, *Envy*. Coleen, her five sisters and two brothers, grew up in a very traditional household, where the girls did all the washing up and hogged the bathroom. As a mum herself, she has noticed an innate difference between the natural behaviour of her daughter Ciara and her two sons Shane Jnr and Jake – but she would sacrifice everything for any one of them.

LISA MAXWELL

Lisa is convinced that men are more competitive than women, and yet she would stop at nothing to win the mums' race at her daughter Beau's sports day! Lisa grew up with her mother and grandparents in the Elephant and Castle, London and won a scholarship to the Italia Conti Academy. Her varied career began when she was a child with a role on TV in a schools programme *A Place Like Home*; at fourteen she made her West End debut as an orphan in the original production of *Annie*. In 1982 she voiced Kira in the Jim Henson film *The Dark Crystal*.

Kids' TV presenting followed, on the ITV show *Splash* and BBC's *No Limits*, after which she became a fixture on the Saturday night comedy scene, regularly working alongside Les Dennis, Russ Abbott, Jasper Carrott and Noel Edmonds, among others. This led to her own BBC sketch show, *The Lisa Maxwell Show*, a contract with Paramount and a three-year spell in Hollywood. She has performed at three Royal Variety Shows and been the subject of Michael Aspel's *This is Your Life*.

Refreshingly frank about all areas of her life, Lisa is very happily unmarried to her partner Paul Jessup – and life has never been better. After seven years playing D.I. Samantha Nixon on the ITV1 drama *The Bill*, since leaving the series she has become a Loose Woman, moved to the countryside and is branching into sitcom.

DENISE WELCH

There's no one quite like Denise! The longest serving wife on the panel (twenty-one years and counting!) this talented actress and adoring mother of two is the daughter of a flamboyant cross dresser. *Loose Women* wouldn't be the same without her unique take on relationships and sex, although hubby Tim would quite possibly sleep easier!

Denise made her name in a range of TV series, including *Spender*, *Coronation Street* and *Waterloo Road*; she is also the author of the unputdownable bestselling autobiography, *Pulling Myself Together*. She fondly remembers her first date with Paul Bean when she was eleven and swears that if she were single, she would never read a dating guide. Q: Would she like to try being a man in bed? A: Is the Pope Catholic?

SHERRIE HEWSON

Gorgeous Sherrie still doesn't know what birds do with bees – and she hasn't a clue how men's minds work. But she has several theories up her sleeve, so it's easy to see why she's such a popular member of the *Loose Women* panel! Sadly, in 2002 Sherrie endured a very painful split from her husband of twenty-six years and she is still struggling with issues of love and trust. But that doesn't mean that she's lost her sense of humour or the quirky and endearing naivety that charms everyone she encounters.

Sherrie's acting career has lasted forty years and she is best known for her roles in *Coronation Street*, *Emmerdale* and *Crossroads*. She is also a talented writer and the author of a crime novel called *The Tannery*. When it comes to love, there is currently only room in her life for her daughter Keeley and grandson Oliver. But in the past she went for every Paul McCartney lookalike she came across, not to mention a raft of young acting students at RADA. And she still absolutely loves a man in uniform, especially RAF officers and polo players!

LYNDA BELLINGHAM

Lovely Lynda spent her entire adolescence in love with one local Aylesbury boy. And yes, she got him in the end, but only after years of yearning agony! When it comes to experience of men, Lynda is hard to beat: at one point in her life, her chat up line was 'I suppose a f***'s out of the question?'; her first husband didn't fancy her and never made love to her; and she got married for the third (and by far the best) time on her sixtieth birthday!

Until she joined *Loose Women* in 2007, Lynda was probably best known as the mum in the OXO gravy ads, although she has since made a big splash in the stage version of *Calendar Girls*. She is also the bestselling author of the funny, moving auto-biography, *Lost and Found*. Her acting career began in the early 1970s with a role in the first daytime soap *General Hospital* and she went on to star in *All Creatures Great and Small* and *Faith in the Future*. She has a wealth of wisdom to impart when it comes to sex and relationships: among other things, she thinks that it just might be a good idea to have sex lessons before you get married! Bring it on!

CAROL MCGIFFIN

Two years ago, Carol was growing weary of her life. After seven years of celibacy, she was planning to move to Paris and shake things up a bit. But then along came Mark and everything changed. Suddenly she found herself falling madly in love with a gorgeous younger man – and virtually the next minute they were engaged!

Carol has always been known to enjoy life, while fearlessly voicing her opinions, come what may. She began her broadcasting career co-hosting a Saturday morning show with Chris Evans, whom she went on to marry (and divorce!) and has since diversified into radio, TV and print journalism. She is also the author of a witty and compelling bestselling memoir, *Oh Carol!*

She is much loved on the show for her brutal honesty and standing up for her sometimes controversial beliefs. She has also visibly softened since she met Mark, it has to be said.

ANDREA MCLEAN

Beautiful Andrea is married to big, burly Steve the builder and they live in Surrey with her two children, Finlay and Amy. She's a strong believer in romance, even if it simply revolves around the telly and a takeaway at home; spontaneity and passion also figure high in her priorities and she finds that there's 'nothing nicer than having a snog thrust upon you when you're in the middle of cooking.' In the nicest possible way, of course. Don't forget, this is 'Snow White' who's talking!

A key anchor on the show, Andrea is a dab hand at keeping the loose ladies in check, marshalling their often conflicting opinions with wit and genial charm. A trained journalist, she spent eleven years getting up at dawn to present the weather on *GMTV*, before opting to concentrate on *Loose Women*, other TV presenting, journalism – and sleeping!

JANE MCDONALD

Witty, down-to-earth Jane loves spooning in bed with her other half Ed Rothe. So why does she insist of having such an enormous bed that you could fit a bus stop in the middle of it? There are certain contradictions to Jane's character that make her opinions especially interesting. For instance, she says that there might be a case for turning a blind eye to infidelity, because there can be much more to a relationship than sex. Who'd have thought it?

A sparkling combination of glamorous diva and Yorkshire lass, Jane started out as a cabaret singer in the industrial north before making her name on the BBC docusoap *The Cruise*. She went on to present BBC's *National Lottery* and ITV's *Star for a Night* before joining *Loose Women* in 2004, just after a very public divorce. It was one of the best decisions of her life and led indirectly to her reunion with true love Ed, whom she had first met and fallen in love with when she was nineteen!

ZOE TYLER

Known for her heartfelt honesty and self-deprecating humour, Zoe admits to having pinned down a few men in her time! When her ex suggested getting married, she said yes, but only on the condition that they got it over quickly and did it in Vegas. She's a woman who knows her own mind!

Born in Portsmouth, brought up in Birmingham and now

firmly established in Essex, Zoe spent thirteen years singing in West End shows like *Les Miserables*, *Joseph*, *City of Angels* and *Fame*. Her TV break came when she was recruited as the vocal coach on the BBC talent show, *How Do You Solve a Problem Like Maria?* She screamed the house down when she was told she'd got a job on *Loose Women* and she's been a brilliant addition to the panel ever since.

KATE THORNTON

A natural in the anchor seat, Kate joined *Loose Women* in 2009 and is a hugely popular addition to the show. After training as a journalist, she started out as an intern at the *Sunday Mirror* and was soon given her own 'youth' column on the *Daily Mirror*. By 21, she was editing the pop magazine *Smash Hits* and it wasn't long before she made the move into TV. She has since presented *Top of the Pops*, *Pop Idol*, *Comic Relief* and the *X Factor*, among other shows.

Kate planned to marry her fiancé Darren in a big ceremony in Tuscany, only to discover that she was pregnant and would be giving birth three weeks after the event! So they're still engaged, and instead of a wedding album they now have Ben, the love of both their lives.

LESLEY GARRETT

Bells started to ring for Britain's most popular soprano when she was introduced to Dr Peter Christian in her dressing room at The Coliseum in London. They instantly fell in love – and the rest is history. A hugely successful opera singer, Lesley has won acclaim for a variety of comic and serious roles, released

13 albums, hosted two TV series and was appointed CBE in 2002. She now lives in north London with Peter and their two children, Jeremy and Chloe.

Lesley isn't bothered if men don't know the small stuff about you, like your bra size and eye colour. What counts, she says, is discussing the big important things, from what you want out of life to the children's futures. She became a regular panellist on the show in spring 2006 and has charmed viewers with her fresh, bubbly take on life and love.

Chapter 1

First impressions

DADDY'S PRINCESSES AND MUMMY'S SOLDIERS

Dads and father figures have a lot to answer for. They're the ones we first look to as we begin to form our opinions of men, so you could say that the example they set is crucial. Or, if the women ruled the roost in your house as you were growing up, you may well dismiss dads as a total irrelevance!

Does it make a difference if your father likes to dress up in women's clothes, though? There's only one Loose Woman who knows the answer to that! Also, if you grew up in a very traditional household, where male and female roles were very defined, are you likely to imitate those customs when you have your own family, or rebel against them?

The way boys and girls differ as they're growing up fascinates us. The assumption that it's always guns and cars for one, and dolls and make-up for the other, doesn't necessarily hold true in our eyes, although it's definitely the norm. Is one sex easier to parent than the other? Well, that depends . . . on whether they've turned into grunting, back-talking teenagers or not! Ah, families!

And then comes the moment when you start to look outside

the home for male companionship, not quite knowing how utterly enthralling this new focus in your life will turn out to be . . .

So, to get us started, we thought we should kick off with the big question, the one that we've spent most of our lives trying to figure out . . .

What makes men tick?

SHERRIE: I haven't the slightest idea! I don't understand what they want out of life or how one man can be so totally different from another – mind you, that goes for women, too. Still, I absolutely love men and I really enjoy their company.

COLEEN: I don't think a woman will ever truly know what makes a man tick, but I think we get close, whereas I don't think men will ever know what makes a woman tick and they don't get near, because they're not really bothered. 'Yeah, whatever, love; just give me an easy ride.'

LISA: Women can't ever fully understand what makes men tick. Trying to work it out is part of the fun. It's the intrigue that keeps us there. Anyway, what would we talk about if we knew what men were thinking and fully understood them? We'd never have another girlie lunch or girls' night out! We'd be able to share everything with men, so we wouldn't have any need for girlfriends. What an appalling thought!

What did your father teach you about men?

LYNDA: I grew up with the perfect example of a man in my father, which was the beginning of all my problems! He was totally upright, a complete hero, a pilot in the war who flew bombers. He had a typical RAF moustache and was very handsome. Reserved, but quite twinkly with it, he didn't talk about his emotions but was very affectionate. As a family, we were always having cuddles. I felt I could talk to my parents about anything.

I suppose I grew up thinking that all men should be like my father. He was very masculine in an era when Cary Grant and Gary Cooper were icons of manhood, and yet he was brilliant with babies. He wasn't a modern man or anything, but you could hand any baby to my father and it would happily look up at his moustache and listen to his very deep voice, without ever crying. There is something about a 'real' man holding a baby that is so sexy and so endearing, isn't there?

I can still remember my father in his BOAC (British Overseas Airways Corporation) pilot's uniform, before he retired early to become a farmer. He used to come back from trips to New York and other long-haul destinations with wonderful presents for my sisters and me. When I was five or six he brought back a perfectly gorgeous dress for me. Even at that young age, I was amazed that my dad was able to pick out such a lovely dress, when it was normally my mum who bought our clothes. He could do that and yet at the same time be such a man.

ANDREA: It sounds like he was in touch with his feminine side. That was also the case with your father, wasn't it, Denise?

DENISE: That's an interesting question to ask the daughter of a known cross-dresser called Raquel! My father has never been afraid to show his feminine side – and I mean that literally! He has never been one to hide his emotions, either. I have seen him cry on more than one occasion and he wouldn't be embarrassed that I said so. He certainly broke down the gender barriers as I was growing up.

He is not remotely a macho man. He loves the company of my gay friends; he enjoys their flamboyancy and sense of humour. He is very comfortable with who he is, to the point that although he is 100 per cent straight, he still thinks nothing of donning a pink evening dress to surprise his friends at a party. And I know he's 100 per cent straight, because he would definitely tell me if that wasn't the case.

My friend Lesley asked him to dress up for a fiftieth birthday party recently. He knew our little circle but he didn't know 90 per cent of the party. Of course because of his personality, he was the toast of the evening!

I haven't really analysed what effect it's had on me to grow up with a dad who likes to dress up as a woman. I've always been quite confident socially and sexually, so I certainly don't think it's done me any harm psychologically. I love men wearing make-up, so there might be a consequence there. Not that I get my husband to wear make-up! Nor do I hang out in bars where men wear make-up, if there are such bars, which I'm sure there are. But I do love a little bit of guy-liner on a man and I am actually quite attracted to men when they drag up a little bit. It's interesting. But I want it to be known here and now that I don't hang out with the ladyboys of Bangkok, desperate for a date!

ANDREA: Things were a little more traditional in your household, weren't they, Coleen?

COLEEN: You could say that! I grew up in the old-fashioned Irish way of men doing very little and women doing all the work. Ten of us lived in a tiny three-bedroom terrace and it always seemed to be the girls in the kitchen: one washing and one drying, after my mum had cooked. The men didn't rule the roost, as such, but they did their jobs and the women did theirs. I don't ever remember the boys being told, 'Right, it's your turn to wash up.' It was always out of the six girls.

And the men always got served first at dinner time. Subconsciously or not, I seem to follow that example: I've noticed that when we all sit down to Sunday dinner or Christmas dinner and I've got family there, I still serve the men their dinner first and I give them more food than I give the women. That's obviously just something I watched and absorbed as I was growing up. Also, like my mother, if I haven't cooked enough, I'll go without. I would never say to my husband or one of my sons, 'I haven't done enough, so you're not having any roast potatoes, because I'm having them.' Having said that, it's only about twice a year that I do cook! I'm not a whizz in the kitchen, I have to say.

One thing that worked against the boys was that they never got to use the bathroom! Can you imagine, with six girls? In fact, I don't ever remember seeing them go in the bathroom. I don't know where they washed or went to the toilet. They just had to get in there when they could, which wasn't often.

Sandra suddenly realised why people had always warned her,
'never marry a man like your father' . . . !

ANDREA: Who was dominant, your mum or dad?

COLEEN: My dad was definitely the disciplinarian but I think my mum actually ruled the roost. Despite there being eight children, things ran smoothly because of my mum. She did everything; she was a very strong woman. When she was in labour, she went on the bus to the hospital, because my dad was at work. In those days, men didn't come in for the birth. My dad just got a phone call to say, 'There's another one! Clear the drawer out.' I really was stuck in a drawer; how bad was that? Not that bad I suppose, as long as they didn't shut it. Maybe that's what happened to me – lack of oxygen! I said, 'I hope I was top drawer, not bottom drawer, Mother!'

My mum was the one that screamed and shouted and chased us with a bamboo cane and yet my dad was the one we were scared of. It's really weird, because he very rarely smacked us. He didn't have to. He would just stand there and look at you and you would die a thousand deaths.

I went to my mum for everything. If I was ill, I wanted my mum. That's how kids are, isn't it? My kids are the same. It's because dads don't take any nonsense, basically. If they tell you to stop it, you stop it, because there are consequences. But Mum will say, 'Stop it!' a thousand times before she batters you.

ANDREA: How about you, Lynda? Was your mum or your dad the household force?

LYNDA: My mother and father were very equal, but they each had their absolute roles. Her role was to make his home comfortable for him and the children; his role was to protect his family and provide for them. My father was head of the household. He dealt with the money. My mother was a housewife. She didn't work, but they always made joint decisions about important things in their lives, so they were good role models.

I remember being very impressed by my parents when Dad was contemplating retirement and pension funds became a big thing. There were financial advisors going around Middle England trying to sell pensions and my mum and dad went to a range of presentations by different fund managers. My mum was not bright in that area at all, but Dad helped her to focus and understand. In this area, they were way ahead of their time.

My big thing now is that I want women to talk openly about being sixty and think through how they are going to spend the rest of their life. You must ask your husband to explain the finances, so that you understand what is going on. Also, you must make a will!

ANDREA: That's very sensible advice. So was there that kind of balance between your parents, Sherrie?

SHERRIE: No, not at all. I grew up in a matriarchal house. It wasn't in the least bit patriarchal. Where was my father? Well, that was debatable. He was a singer, so he was always out and about somewhere. I loved him desperately, but my mother ran the household and was the power within the home. That's why I've grown up to be so strong as a woman, I think.

We had an enormous house; my father lived in his bit and my mother lived in her bit and then they came together. My role models were all women: my mother, my grandmother and my great-grandmother, who lived until she was ninety-nine. My brother went to boarding school when he was seven years old, so I didn't see him very much.

Growing up in a household where women dominated probably instilled in me the capacity to be everything in this world, to play both the man's and the woman's roles in life. I was on the stage from the age of four, so I had to be strong, although my mother was always there behind me and I guess that gave me confidence.

My father was the most loving person in the world. There was no man lovelier than my father, but we were a tight matriarchal circle and he just got on with life. He was a free spirit and lived like a bird, flying where he wanted and doing what he wanted. He was always happy because he was free. Women absolutely adored him.

My mum was a beautiful model. She worked for the House of Orlane, in Paris. Perhaps she was such a big personality because of that. My father worked and provided, but my mother also worked and provided. She was the person who drove me and kept me driven and working; she made sure I stayed on the straight and narrow.

ANDREA: So how did the men in your family shape your idea of men and masculinity, Sherrie?

SHERRIE: No man could measure up to either my father or my brother, for me. My father was unconditionally loving. He loved me beyond belief. It wouldn't have mattered if I'd killed fifty people, he'd still have said, 'Don't worry, we will find a way out of this. I'll sort it.'

My brother was a beautiful boy, absolutely stunning, and still is. He went on to be a very successful model and looked similar to Robert Redford. I always thought I knew him, just because he was my brother, but I suppose I didn't, because he was away for most of my childhood. When he came home at long last, he went straight out again into the world. Like my father, he is a free spirit, but someone who has always known what he wants and a workaholic with it. He has a bar in Conwy, Wales; he got everything he wanted. I still look up to him and think, 'How fantastic to be a man like that!'

But my brother and father weren't central figures in my life because my mother was the powerhouse of the family. I grew up thinking that women rule; I don't think I've ever stopped believing that women run everything, while making men believe that they have all the power.

My mother was incredibly industrious. She ran everything in the house, worked and started businesses. The house was always a hive of activity and she was constantly thinking of new projects. 'Let's do this; let's do that and make some money,' she'd say. At one point she started breeding beautiful black and white poodles in the out houses down the garden. The idea came to her because she would often model posed with a black and a white poodle.

My mother's power seemed to extend even into the enormous garden, where the roses were all in a line and possessed the biggest heads you've ever seen in your life. They even blossomed when they should; they had no choice!

Her power and self-control were passed on to my brother and me as children. I thank God for it, because that's what has got me through life. I've also partly inherited my father's fey side. I'm always saying, 'I live in my own world.' Sometimes

I need a wake-up call to bring me back into this world, though, and I come back with a bang. On the other hand, I'm a workaholic like my mother and my brother and I can be totally focused, so I have both of my parents in me.

ANDREA: What about you, Lisa? Did one sex rule in your household as you were growing up, and did that shape your idea of men?

LISA: I grew up in a house with my mother, my grandmother and my grandfather, so I had three parents, in a sense. My mum had me 'out of wedlock', as it was called in the early 1960s so we lived with her parents in their flat in the Elephant and Castle.

My nan definitely ruled the roost. I always felt she was in charge; she was in charge of my mum as well, which was always a bone of contention between my mother and me, because it meant we were more like sisters. My nan had such a strong personality and my mum struggled with her role in my life as a result.

My granddad hardly ever said anything, but if he spoke, it made an impact. If us three women were bickering, things would have to develop into a proper slanging match before my granddad said, 'Will you please just shut up?' That did it; we'd all shut up and crawl away. So although I always thought my nan had the upper hand, perhaps secretly my granddad did. He just didn't feel he had to prove it to anybody.

ANDREA: So how did he form your idea of what a man was, or should be?

LISA: Back then, I had a very different impression to the one I have now of what a man should be like. My granddad was from the next generation back, so I grew up thinking that men just didn't get involved in women's things; you didn't have heart-to-heart conversations with men. A man didn't talk about his feelings or change nappies. He came home from work to find his dinner on the table and didn't even make a cup of tea for himself.

Interestingly, I now live with a man who is totally in touch with his feelings and is incredibly sensitive and open. It's impractical for my generation of women to be with a man like my granddad. You can't go through life without sharing your feelings with your partner and sharing childcare! But I never saw my grandfather do anything remotely domestic. Women cooked and looked after babies. Men went to work and put money on the table.

ANDREA: So your grandmother didn't have a job?

LISA: Actually, she did, because there wasn't enough money. Funnily enough, I never questioned that, and as far as I know, neither did she. Granddad had this stereotypical view of a woman as the housekeeper and yet as well as all that housework, Nan had to get up every morning and go office cleaning with him. My poor nan!

Back then, a woman couldn't bring up a family on her own. She didn't have that option. I'm glad that we have more choice now and yet there's a part of me that wonders if we've over-complicated things and expect too much of men. It's really hard to find somebody to live up to all our expectations nowadays.

My nan didn't expect anything from my granddad. I remember her saying, 'He's a bloody good man, your grand-dad. He's never raised a hand to me.' That's kind of dark and dysfunctional, but it worked for her. I don't think I was in a position to turn round and say, 'Actually, that's not right, Nan!' It would have been very patronising of me. It was their life; they lived it the way they lived it and it worked for them. When he died, she missed him dreadfully.

Are boys different from girls from the very start?

DENISE: I'm very interested in the concepts of nature and nurture. I've got two boys and I've been part of my nieces' upbringing, so I've seen both sides, to some extent. My boys wanted to watch *Thomas the Tank Engine* and play with cars and guns from day one. Neither of them would have been persuaded to play with a doll, whereas my sister's girls always wanted to play with dolls. It was something innate, because I would have fought their corner if the boys had wanted to play with Barbie – and so would my father!

All the kids are totally accepting of their grandpa. Both my sister and I have children who seem to be without any preju-dice whatsoever, which is really nice. Maybe it's something to do with growing up with their slightly different grandfather and that being a very normal thing.

ANDREA: And did you play with dolls, Denise?

DENISE: Yes, but for some reason I was never allowed Barbie or Sindy. I always had to have Tressie, which felt like second best! She had the hair that grew when you pressed a button. It was obviously much more original and I get that now, but as a child I just wanted to conform and have Barbie and Sindy. Maybe Tressie had an effect, though. Maybe she's why I go from having short hair for six months to getting extensions put in and then whipping them out. Perhaps it's all because of Tressie.

LISA: It's interesting that my daughter Beau doesn't give a hoot about make-up and hair. I think it's because Paul looked after her for many years while I was in *The Bill*, so she's had a lot of male influence and is very much one of the boys, even though she's absolutely gorgeous. She's never been a girly girl. She has a very male sense of humour; she laughs at fart jokes. She loves insects.

DENISE: So she wasn't interested in dolls?

LISA: She likes dolls, actually. She started going through a 'playing mummy' phase when she was about eight. At one point she bought a real car seat for her baby doll and we'd have to go round Mothercare and buy clothes for the doll. I don't know where that came from! It worried me a bit. At one point I was thinking, 'She's really into this baby thing. Maybe when she's sixteen she's going to have a teenage pregnancy!'

I've never been particularly maternal. As a child I used to think that having babies was revolting and bad news, because of the way I came into the world, to a single mother. I only really remember playing with Sindy, which was more of a fashion doll. Actually, I did have a Tiny Tears, but I don't remember being particularly bothered about it.

DENISE: For me, Tiny Tears and Tressie were the two loves of my life. I was always desperate to have babies, from a very young age. As I grew up I wasn't remotely interested in boys' things like cars and football; they leave me completely cold. I mean, I'm not like Katie Price, I'm not Jordan-esque in that pink way, but I don't have that tomboy element in me. Mind you, at fifty-two, I have just bought a pair of dungarees. Make of that what you will!

LYNDA: I'm sure you look very feminine in them! It's an interesting area, isn't it. My sister, who had two daughters, once gave my youngest son Robbie a toy vacuum cleaner as a present. 'Why are you giving him a vacuum cleaner?' I asked. 'Because he needs to be in touch with his feminine side,' she replied. Well, he simply looked at this vacuum and looked away. It was never even touched.

He did go through a period of having a baby girl doll, for about six months, though. It had a bottle and he fed it and absolutely adored it. I thought that was great and I encouraged it. Other people reacted by saying, 'Maybe he's insecure. Obviously something is worrying him.' That struck me as a pretty negative reaction. I suppose some people may have wondered about his sexuality, but it didn't even cross my mind that I should worry.

Apart from the doll episode, both my boys were very boyish. I remember we went to the countryside to visit my sister, God bless her. She had opted out of London after living in Clapham for years, working as a really feisty photographer, very front line and urban living. Now she was in the countryside and she had a son and a daughter. One of my sons was playing with her son and being boyish, tumbling around, like boys do. 'Oh, it's terrible to see that urban aggression,' said my sister. 'What?' I said, astounded. They were just being boys!

I was very nervous when I was pregnant with my first child and found out he was a boy, because I knew nothing about boys. We were all girls in my family. What would I do with his willy? The minute you change that nappy, you are literally faced with the fact that your child is not a girl!

As it turned out, I loved having boys. There is a special relationship between mothers and sons, because you are different sexes. Your little boys are so affectionate to you when they're young! One son used to play with my hair every time he had a drink. It was wonderful. The terrible thing is that it stops. You wake up one day, when they're about twelve, and it stops.

Having sons can be very difficult for women who go through a relationship split. When I was on my own, I really had to fight the desire to have them in the bed and cuddle them and use them emotionally, because they give you so much love and you feel so wanted. It doesn't seem to be the same with girls and their mothers.

LISA: One of my mum's friends was a single parent with a son. I remember my mum saying how protective of her he was. He was her 'little man'. And I have a friend who has an only child who is a boy; when she divorced, her son slept in her bed until quite a grown-up age, something like ten or eleven, maybe older.

LYNDA: That's what I tried very hard not to do, really.

ANDREA: Coleen, you've got boys and a girl. Have you seen a noticeable difference between them?

COLEEN: Bringing up boys is totally different to bringing up girls. From an early age, boys' play is much more aggressive, as Lynda says. In my experience, they'll be wrestling and somersaulting off the bed at every opportunity, while a girl is happy to sit and colour in a picture.

LYNDA: I can't stand it when little girls go through that girly phase, when they flirt with everybody. Boys are much more simple. 'I don't like you!' they say. They are much more honest. I really enjoy all their games. We used to play wrestling and my bedroom became a WWE wrestling ring!

COLEEN: Yes, boys and girls definitely have different tastes from a very early age. I think it's something innate, even now that times have changed so much. The kids' cartoons that are aimed at boys, like *X-Men* and *Power Rangers*, are quite aggressive. They're all about fighting and saving the world. With girls it's all Fifi and the Flowertots and Dora the Explorer. Men are still programmed to be the hunters and women to be the nurturers.

ANDREA: Is one sex easier than the other, then?

COLEEN: Well, some of my friends who have both sexes say, 'Give me boys over girls anytime! They're so much easier.' But it's been the other way round for me. I don't know whether that's because

'I leave them for five minutes, come back and Gemma has built a fairy castle, while Jamie has built a . . . well, it looks like it might be a nuclear explosion'

my last one is a girl, so I'm a different parent now. Maybe if she had been the first one, she might have been more difficult. As babies and toddlers, the boys were harder for me. But they were great as teenagers, so perhaps teenage girls are harder.

·I never really had any problems with the boys as teenagers. Of course, there was an element of the Kevin and Perry, and sometimes Jake was Kevin and Perry all in one. With me, he was shoulders down, grunting; when other people came round, he'd be, 'Yes, thank you, Mrs Patterson!' People would say, 'He's so lovely and polite!' Really? I'd think. He just grunts at me. But basically, if they wanted to grunt and walk off to their rooms, I just let them get on with it.

DENISE: That's pretty much my approach as well.

COLEEN: When it comes to disciplining children, I've never understood 'grounding', unless I can ground them at someone else's house. When my sons were naughty, my friend used to say, 'Just ground them for a week!' 'I don't want them in the house for a week, thank you!' I'd say. 'That's just punishing me!' So then I used to say to the boys, 'If you're not careful, I'm going to ground you − round at my friend Carol's house!'

Did you ever want to be a boy?

COLEEN: I never wanted to be a boy when I was a child. I'd have hated to be a boy.

DENISE: I was never a tomboy. I still love girliness and femininity.

LISA: I didn't want to be a boy either, but I often wondered if my mum wished that I was a boy, because she didn't have a husband or a boyfriend. I thought that if I were a boy, I could be the man in her life. It was something I worked out early on. I think my mum would have liked a son. She may say differently nowadays, but maybe there was a time when she might have wished for one.

I wouldn't say I was ever a tomboy. I wouldn't say I was a young temptress, either, because I didn't have the tools with which to be one. I always looked very young for my age because I was very small. I was paying half fare on the Tube until I was about 24, maybe even older. When I was eleven, I looked about five!

LYNDA: I often wished I was a boy when I was in my teens. It looked much easier to be a boy. They seemed to be more independent and have more straightforward choices. It was easier for them to do what they wanted to do. I couldn't see how as a girl I could have an acting career, which was all I cared about. I certainly never thought about children – I thought having kids would ruin my chances to act. I remember years later Meryl Streep saying, 'It's very tough on women.'

DENISE: It must be the way I've been brought up, but I've never felt that I couldn't do anything as well as a man could, or that my chances have been limited because I'm a woman. I've never really thought in those terms.

LYNDA: Yes, but you must admit that the minute you have children, you are a different person altogether. So you either have to avoid becoming a mother or accept that, when you do, it's the end of your career and your ambition for a while. If you are lucky enough to come back to it, that's terrific. Had I really understood that, I think I may have chosen to have my children early on. Get them out of the way and then go into acting in my thirties.

DENISE: Well, strangely enough, my TV career only took off around a year after I'd had my first child. That's when I was offered two TV series at once – and I accepted them both!

Do girls mature quicker than boys?

COLEEN: I don't know whether girls actually mature quicker than boys or just play at being mature, by getting into fashion and hair and make-up while boys remain sporty and wanting to play football. I don't know if it's maturity or just a gender thing. What did my mum and dad say? 'Look, she's smelling herself!' Every time he caught me looking in the mirror, my dad would say, 'Stop smelling yourself.'

LISA: Lovely! I think it's true that girls mature faster in the early days. Girls play in a less physical way than boys, which is what makes you think they're more cerebral and maybe their brains are a bit more advanced. But I think that changes. Boys and girls learn differently and I'm a big believer in single-sex schools, especially for girls. Boys need to be competitive. And isn't it a proven fact that they have different brains, in terms of learning about mathematics and English?

I've chosen a single-sex school for Beau, based on the fact that she's been in co-ed since she was two, so she knows what a boy looks like and she's had a very male-dominated upbringing to date. I think that during puberty, boys are a distraction. I think it's the same for boys: they're so self-conscious when girls are around. So it's probably better if you separate them during those years when they're supposed to be learning the stuff that's going to make them into adults, during the most intense part of their education, from eleven onwards. Girls learn better when they're not worried about what the boys are going to think when they want to express themselves about a piece of literature. I think boys would flourish more without girls around, too.

When did you first start getting interested in boys?

LISA: My earliest memory of liking a boy was on a primary school trip to Norfolk when I was ten. He was a blond boy and I think his name was Gary. (I've always liked blond boys; Paul's blond.) 'Tiger Feet' by Mud was playing at the school disco and I danced as close as I could to him, with my hands on my hips, doing the 'Tiger Feet' dance, which probably didn't do anything for him. Forever after, my pulling technique was always to dance close to a boy, because I fancied myself as quite a good mover, and still do!

I really liked Gary. I thought that if I borrowed my

friend Wendy's 'edge-to-edge' cardigan, he would really notice me. An edge-to-edge cardigan was a long, thin-knit, belted cardigan that met in the middle. It seemed so posh to me, because I was used to a home knit, a chunky knit or a Starsky and Hutch knit. Wendy wouldn't lend it to me, but I took it anyway and put it on. I felt like the bee's knees in front of Gary wearing that cardigan! He didn't really notice me and nothing came of it, but it was a lot of fun having him there as a focus. It added extra pizzazz to the school trip!

It's funny to think that I was the same age as my daughter Beau is now. She's generally much more aware of boys than I was, I think. I was small and fairly underdeveloped until quite late on – and I never stopped being small – so boys never fancied me, although I got on great with them because I made them laugh. I had mousy hair and a bit of a sticky eye thing going on. I think it must have been conjunctivitis, but we didn't do doctors in my family. As I've said to my mum on many occasions, she neglected my health! But Beau is very glamorous and she's developing more quickly than I did.

I remember going for my first job, which was *Ballet Shoes*. They needed a classroom of eleven-year-old kids who were less than four foot six. Well, I was barely four foot! When the agency asked whether I was less than four foot six, my mum said, 'Hang on, I'll have to measure her.' I was four foot one and when my mum told them, I actually heard a roar of laughter from the agent down the phone. 'She can do the job, then!'

Boys at that age want girls that look older, don't they? With boobs. But I was wearing my 30 AA junior bra up until the age of about twenty. It was peppermint green from Marks and Spencer. I remember it as if it was yesterday.

COLEEN: I was always a bit scared of boys because I was brought up so strictly. When we were younger, my sisters and I weren't even allowed boys from school at our birthday parties; it was all girls. For my older sisters, that was a rule that extended past teenage years! But by the time it got to me, my dad seemed to have given up. I think he thought, 'You know what? She's the eighth kid; I don't care!'

I probably started getting interested in boys from the age of twelve or thirteen, but if they ever went to kiss me, that was it! I hated that. It scared me to death. Then I fell deeply in love at fifteen and went from hating the idea of being kissed to being in a full-blown relationship. He was the first person I kissed – and the rest. I went out with him for four years.

I matured very quickly at fifteen when I joined my sisters and went from being a normal schoolkid to touring the world and being surrounded by adults. Emotionally, I felt like I grew up almost overnight. Looking back, I maybe wasn't that mature, but then again, I reckon I probably was compared to the fifteen-year-olds I see nowadays. They just seem to have no idea of anything!

SHERRIE: I was a very late developer when it came to boys and I have been very naive all my life. Relationships were never very important to me. All I knew was that I wanted to get married and have a baby, without knowing when or how I was going to do it.

I didn't start to go on dates until quite late on, partly because I was on the stage all the time, travelling around doing revues. My days and nights were often taken up with rehearsing, dancing and singing; I was always being fitted for a tutu or appearing in a show. That was my whole teenage life really, until I went to RADA (the Royal Academy of Dramatic Arts) at eighteen.

I played Anita in *West Side Story* when I was fifteen and won the Laurence Olivier Award for Best Newcomer. The show went from Nottinghamshire to London to the Minnack Theatre in Cornwall and then back to London. So I led a theatrical life and there was no time for boys. I didn't have that normal experience of going to school, meeting a boy and going out with him.

Also, boys didn't matter to me for a long time because when I wasn't on stage, I lived for my horses. I wanted to live *with* them too and often slept in the stables. First I had an enormous horse called a Garrano, which had a stripe down the back of its body. Then I had a tiny racehorse called Whisky. He grew, but I never raced him. I rode from a very early age and fear didn't even cross my mind until I was seventeen, when I was thrown very badly, unfortunately. Once fear sets in, a horse can immediately sense it, and that's when my riding came to a stop.

My brother used to take me to late-night parties and I'd think, I don't like this, I really don't. I used to get lots of attention, but I didn't enjoy it and I would back away if anyone tried to kiss me. I don't know quite why. 'Don't start that with me!' I'd warn them. I remember once going to a party with my brother in our village, Burton Joyce in Nottinghamshire. My brother was made to take me because

I supposedly wanted to go. At 11 p.m. I was asleep on the settee and Brett had to take me home. He never forgave me for that, because mum wouldn't let him go back to the party, where he must have been getting off with a girl!

COLEEN: Oh dear! That must have been a blow for a teenage boy!

Chapter 2

Getting to know you . . .

'PUT ON LIONEL RICHIE AND LET'S HAVE A SMOOCH'

Pre-teen dates, church discos, hanging around cafés after school waiting for *him* to walk in; does anyone have any idea of what they're doing at this early stage in the mating game? And can anyone remember how they learnt about the birds and bees?

Those early milestones mean so much, don't they? The first crush, the first flirty conversation, that very first snog with tongues . . . It's easy to cringe looking back – at what he wore and what you said and how your heart leapt at every smouldering glance he gave you – but would you have had it any other way (not counting David Cassidy and Paul McCartney fantasies!)?

As life goes on, dating is supposed to become a far more sophisticated ritual, but in fact continues to throw up disasters along the way. Not fancying your date can be a real setback; and if he lets one off at the table it doesn't exactly set the romantic dream scene either! But are men and women actually looking for different things in a relationship? If so, how on earth do we manage to stay with each other for more than a few days? (Clues: wine, sex, the temporary madness of infatuation.)

First of all, though, you have to find him and meet him. Strangely, it's not as easy as it sounds!

What about your very first date?

DENISE: The first date that I can remember going on was with my first boyfriend, Paul, when I was eleven. It was an arranged date, as opposed to just hanging out by chance or going behind the bike sheds, and my parents picked me up and ensured that I was brought home afterwards. But for the date we just walked around the estate where he lived! We held hands and with my spare hand I pushed along a little pram thing that you pushed along a wall. It was a bit naff, but I loved it. My sister was going out with Paul's brother, Sidney, so sometimes we went on double dates, both with our prams.

It was all very exciting. I thought I was in love with Paul. I only realised I wasn't in love with him when I snogged somebody else at a church disco, while wearing a horrendous multicoloured cord outfit my mother had put me in. Debbie and I had matching cord outfits with coordinating head-scarves. Terrible!

I snogged with tongues for the first time when I was thirteen, with a boy called Andrew. We had a right old tumble in a barn that I'll never forget. It was still quite innocent stuff, even though I knew where that kind of behaviour could lead and that it was something that in the future I wanted to be part of. I was never shocked when boys tried to take things a step further, but I was the one who decided.

SHERRIE: You were so different to me, Denise! Sex passed me by when I was younger. I wasn't that physical; I wasn't bothered one way or the other.

Having said that, when I was a girl, there was a pop duo called Paul and Barry Ryan; they were very pretty boys and I have always been into pretty boys. One was prettier than the other and I really liked him, so when I met a boy who looked like him, around the age of twelve, I really fell for him. I didn't see him for a couple of years and then he telephoned my house and asked me to the cinema, when I was about fourteen. Remembering how gorgeous he had been, I agreed to go.

I went to meet him, but just before I arrived at the cinema, I thought, 'I'll just have a look at him first.' So I sort of sneaked up, trying not to get too close so he'd see me. Oh no, where had the pretty boy gone? He had turned into a chubby, spotty teenager, so I just ran away. How cruel is that? He never rang again. He must have seen me taking a peek.

Why do teenage girls like pretty boys? Well, if you are living in my world, which is Disneyland, you grow up with the Cinderella syndrome. Cinderella met a prince; she didn't meet a frog! So as a girl you think that you're going to marry a prince and have beautiful children. Of course, when you grow up, that's when you meet the frogs.

I always thought Robert Redford was the most beautiful man. I know he is losing it a bit now, but when he was younger he was so stunningly beautiful. Cary Grant was the one perfect man in my life, though. That face!

Mind you, who was the real Cary Grant, or Archie Leach as he was really called? You never knew. According to a book I read the other day, there was always a part of him that remained elusive. Even Cary Grant said that he didn't know who he really was. 'I wish I was Cary Grant,' he once said wistfully. Really, he was Archie Leach and he liked sausages and mash, fish and chips and a beer, not champagne cocktails like Cary Grant. He could never be the man women wanted him to be. 'I'm moody. I'm miserable,' he said. No one actually got near to him. You got close, but you never saw who he really was. His relationships always failed. But in those days you didn't hear much about the private lives of celebrities and stars, so it didn't matter so much. People just wanted the illusion. Now we see every bit of their bodies, every step of their failures, even though nobody really wants to see real people. That's why glossy magazines sell. We don't want reality, do we? We want an illusion. God we need it.

LISA: My first real crush was on David Cassidy, when I was seven or eight. I cried real tears over him. My babysitter took me to see him at Wembley. I was on her shoulders and he came down from the stage and gave me a rose. It was incredible! I remember crying when I saw him on the news in his Yeti boots and pale blue jeans, going in a boat up the Thames. I was really cross that they'd put him in the middle of the water, so that no one could get to him!

Like you, Sherrie, I liked pretty boys and Californian beach types. David had that fabulous feather-cut hair, tiny hips in really faded jeans and a distressed beige suede jacket with fringing. He had an amazing smile with a slightly crooked tooth and the slightly crooked tooth made all the difference, in the same way that John Lennon had that funny little tooth at the front that made his mouth sexy.

I finally met David Cassidy at a party when I lived in California. I was about 29; I wasn't fully formed as a grown up, so I could still be in the David zone, but he was so small and I don't like small men! Of course, when I was little, he was really big, but now he was tiny, and those little hips that I liked in the pale blue jeans weren't appealing anymore. He seemed to have a really big head and tiny jeans. I was really disappointed.

In some ways, this industry is great, because you get to meet your idols, but in other ways, it absolutely kills it! I regret that, because when I talk about how much I loved David Cassidy, I then have to say, 'And then I met him,' and I wish that my meeting him story was so much better than it is!

I've gone on loving pretty boys because somehow they're less threatening, as I know Sherrie thinks too, although I can completely get Marlon Brando, too. But then Marlon Brando is special. Equally, I can get George Clooney, who is very manly. But my type is really the preppy boy and always has been. There's something about a bloke with a foppish good head of hair and a cable knit thrown around his shoulders. I don't know why, but it gets me every time!

I don't do fat. Isn't that awful? I think it's because I'm so small. It's not like I haven't met overweight men who have been charming and appealing. Perhaps I would just feel self-conscious: skinny little me walking down the road with a big fat bloke. Or maybe it's the thought of being crushed! I'd have to work twice as hard, because I'd be on top all the time, wouldn't I?

SHERRIE: It doesn't bear thinking about! So when – and who – was your first date?

LISA: My first ever date was with a guy who was one of the Lost Boys in *Peter Pan* at the Shaftesbury Theatre. I was sixteen and at stage school at the time. I turned up done up to the nines. *Quadrophenia* had just come out and I was wearing one of my nan's old black and white check wool suits that had been taken in professionally and tapered to fit me. I had white lipstick and a copper tint bob that hung over one eye, Veronica Lake-style; I was up for it! I was putting out properly that night! He was posh and his name was Harvey. We had our first snog and a fiddle in the Royal Box! I think it was the end-of-the-run party and we snuck off and had a bit of a grope.

SHERRIE: Was that really your first date?

LISA: No not really, I wish! It was with a newspaper boy called Lee, who worked at the Elephant and Castle. My friend Danielle and I used to walk past him every day when we came home from school. He was a bit of a cheeky chappie, as you would imagine a newspaper vendor to be. I can't remember much about the date, just that he was wearing a beige suede bomber jacket. There's a beige suede theme developing here that's making me sound a bit like a fetishist! I'd only ever seen him in jeans and sports T shirts, so it was a nice surprise. He had gold jewellery on as well. He was like a little squashed Mike Reid!

COLEEN: He sounds lovely! I didn't have my first actual date until after my first relationship ended. It wasn't very success-ful. He was a friend of my brother's; he chatted me up and said, 'Do you want to go out next Friday?' So I said, 'Yeah, OK.'

He was a nice guy. I liked him, but I absolutely hated the whole date thing. I dreaded it all day. I was so angry at myself for saying yes. I felt mortified and went through every single thing in my wardrobe and in my sisters' wardrobes. That whole idea of him coming round at eight freaked me out and embarrassed me. I kept thinking, I can't bear this!

In fact, once he turned up and we went out, we had a really good night, even though he took me to see Freddie Starr! He (not Freddie) made me laugh all night, but it didn't progress. We'd known each other too long through my brother; we were too much like good mates.

Who was your first love?

LYNDA: When I was twelve I fell in love with a boy called Karel. I was obsessed with him right through into my early twenties. He couldn't have been more different from my father, who was still in some ways my ideal man, but I think maybe that was right at that age. My father represented what grown ups did; his was the life you aspired to, but I wasn't going to waste my time trying to aspire to it yet because I was focusing on becoming an actress. Then suddenly I was faced with teenage love and lust. It overwhelmed me. Karel was sixteen, which meant that there was quite a big age gap between us, although it seemed to narrow as the years went on and had almost disappeared by the time I was sixteen and he was twenty.

This was the time of the mods and the rockers; Karel didn't fit either category exactly, but he leaned toward the mods. He

'Now you show me yours.'
Deborah had always been a bit of a one

was studying at Wycombe Art College; he was an art student, but not a hairy art student, and he went around with a terribly trendy group. I think they represented 'being bad' for me. They were everything I was not.

The group included an amazingly beautiful girl called Sheila, who had classic Marianne Faithful long blonde hair and wore thick black eye make-up. Karel was beautiful too; he was half Czechoslovakian and so very olive skinned with black hair.

I went to Regent Coffee Bar in Aylesbury every day in the hope of meeting Karel, who usually came in at around 5.40p.m. This involved making up a legion of excuses for missing the first bus after school, which went at half past four and got me home by just gone five. If I missed the half past four, I could catch the five o'clock, but it meant I had to walk two miles at the other end, which wasn't good news; I had to wait until 6.10p.m. to get the next bus that would take me to the gate of my house. Catching the 6.10p.m. bus of course meant that I could go to the coffee shop and see Karel, so I became endlessly inventive in my reasons for missing the half past four bus! I've since worked out that I must have spent over 2,000 hours of my life in the Regent Coffee Bar, with my one cup of coffee every time.

It was a long, narrow place with 1960s plastic bench banquettes arranged around fixed tables. As you walked in there was an espresso machine at the daylight end of the room; I always went along to the dark section at the back, which had four tables along each wall. I sat there so that I could see Karel arrive; I just can't put into words the excitement I felt when he came sauntering in. My heart leapt!

Then I'd have at least five minutes to watch him as he stopped to speak to people at every single table as he made his way to the back of the shop. This was his kingdom. If it was my turn to be blessed with his magical presence, he'd come to my table and sit in my banquette. I'd talk endlessly for the next twenty minutes before I had to leave to catch my bus. I always talk a lot when I'm nervous. One day my mother came looking for me and I hid under the table! For years, any kind of outing I had would somehow involve getting to the coffee bar in Aylesbury, because I knew that at some point Karel would come in. When I look back I think, what a weird life he led. He hovered around his little kingdom before going out every night.

Seeing him out of context, away from the coffee bar, was quite strange. I'll never forget the time a boy in the next village asked me out to a party at a pub in High Wycombe. Like Karel, this boy was also an art student. My mother said, 'Well, I will have to come and pick you up.' I was like, 'Oh, for God's sake, Mother!' I must have been 15 or 16. 'Twist and Shout' had just come out and I have this amazing memory of everybody in the pub singing, 'Ah, aah, aaaaah . . . !' The floor was jumping. Then I looked up and Karel was there! I hadn't expected to see him. The whole evening suddenly took on a completely different hue. Of course, I no longer wanted to know the poor bloke who had asked me to the party.

My mother had said she would pick me up in her open-backed mini van. 'OK,' I said, 'But please wait for me around the corner!' When the party ended at pub closing time, everyone started saying, 'Christ, how are we going to get back to Aylesbury?' I turned to Karel and out of my mouth came the words, 'You can have a lift. My mum is round the corner.' 'Great!' he said. The next thing I knew, half the party had found its way into the back of the mini van. I was Miss Cool for a minute and everybody was ferried back. But then off Karel went into the middle of the night with everybody else. I was left with the bloke from the next village and my mum, thank God. For once, I was really pleased she was there!

Over the four or five years that I was in love with him, it would be my turn to go out with Karel every now and then. Going out with him meant trailing behind him, dressed in whatever he thought you should wear. Right from the start, I was walking the fine line between desire to please and having no self-worth.

'You are going to be really gorgeous when you grow up,' he told me, when he first noticed me. 'What you need to do is this . . . Don't wear that; wear this.' He was just so cool and I was so young. I was desperate to fit in. All I really wanted was to be painted by him. But I realised very early on that Sheila was his dream, his muse. Since there was no way I was ever going to be blonde and gorgeous like she was, it was all slightly confusing.

Every summer a number of French girls would come over on exchange visits and Karel would always fall madly in love with one of them. So every year, for a month, I would sort of die quietly. I've actually got a photograph of me in the corner of some party or another, almost in tears as Karel dances with a petite French girl in the foreground. I remember I just wanted to be sick. In a sense, once he had won you, he wasn't interested anymore.

I was definitely obsessed with him, but perhaps more

importantly I wanted a resolution to the situation. I wanted him to go out with me. I wanted us to either fall in love and live happily ever after or for the whole thing to be over. He was still in my mind when I went to drama school; it carried on until I had to accept that it wasn't going anywhere. It was the same with my first and second husbands. I carried on trying longer than other people would because it's in my nature to keep on until there is nowhere else to go.

We did eventually have one night together, a totally unsatisfactory night in my single bed in my flat in London. It was an afterthought, coming long after the height of my obsession with him, but I suppose in my head I had finally achieved what I'd set out to do. Because there had been such a long gap between the time when I was passionately in love with him and the actual act, there was finally nowhere else to go. It wasn't so wonderful that it ignited the passion. So then I accepted it. 'OK, fine. On to the next thing!'

COLEEN: Wow, that's an amazing story, Lynda. My first love was part of the Nolan Sisters tour, one of the musicians, and he was twenty-three. My parents didn't know that I was going out with him until I was seventeen, even though I was seeing him from when I was fifteen. I was just very lucky that he was on tour with us.

Did he set a type in my love life? Well, I went from him to another musician, then I married Shane, who was in the business, then I married a musician! I've only ever been out with one normal guy, someone I met in Blackpool. He was a university student by day and a nightclub bouncer by night.

SHERRIE: Falling in love and sex seemed like very different things to me. I remember absolutely falling in love and wanting to be Doris Day. I've always believed that I'm like Doris Day.

Doris Day has had a very strange life. Her third husband took everything from her but she still managed to present herself as a wholesome, happy, wonderful person, despite all the underlying tragedy in her life. You never saw her sad or crying or admitting anything of what was really going on. I think of myself as similar to her because I might go home now and cry over what has happened to me, but I would never do it in public. I admit my feelings, but I don't show them, because I think I'd be a mess if I started doing that. I wouldn't survive if I broke down and started saying, 'But you don't know what I'm going through!' What's inside has to stay inside.

Again, this is something that comes from my mother. She did a lot of character building with me. I remember falling in love with a boy who looked like Paul McCartney, when I was around thirteen. All we ever did was hold hands; I don't think he even kissed me. I had a fixation on Paul McCartney then, and still do. I've always fallen in love with anyone who looks like him.

One day this boy told me that he didn't want to see me anymore. I absolutely wanted to die. Back at home, I went in to see my mother, who was in bed with some kind of flu. 'I'm very sorry,' she said, when I told her what had happened. Then her tone became stern. 'Right, stop now. It's gone, over. Time to move on.' This jolted me out of my misery. 'OK,' I whimpered. I went out of the room and cried a bit more, but her approach helped me get over it quite quickly and has helped me in everything I've subsequently been through. After a cry at home, I'll say to myself, 'Right, that's enough of that. Get on with the rest of your life.'

That's how I tend to cope with the men in my life. I have this attitude of, 'You can get so close but you are not coming any nearer, or you will have to go.' I'm not sure whether that has actually worked in my favour or not, as I'm on my own!

COLEEN: But the Paul McCartney lookalike wasn't your first real love, was he, Sherrie?

SHERRIE: No, my first love was a wonderful ballet dancer called Freddie. I met him before I went to RADA. We did musicals and shows together all over the country. He went on to the Royal Ballet School but he didn't stay there because Nureyev would never leave him alone. He was beautiful, blond, with big blue eyes. In the end he couldn't cope with all the attention so he ran away and joined the army. He came to see me at RADA, but I'd already met Bob Lindsay by then. I fell in love with Bob straight away, because I was just eighteen and he was playing Romeo.

I fell for all sorts of people at RADA. When I first arrived, Leigh Lawson, who years later ended up marrying Twiggy, showed us round and I instantly fell for him. I just thought he was so beautiful, I couldn't get over it. It was the first time I had been away from home and I was a very young eighteen-year-old so I pretty much fell in love with everybody I met. Actors tend to be pretty and everyone I met could act, so they all seemed very attractive to me. It was like being in a sweet shop.

There was a gorgeous boy called Gavin in my year. I was so in love with him, it wasn't true. Except of course I wasn't really, I just thought I was! He was a guitar-playing hippy type and had masses of curly hair; funnily enough, *Hair* the musical had recently opened in the West End, so it was probably 1969. I thought it was wonderful the way he always had a guitar with him. I wouldn't now – it's funny what you fall for.

COLEEN: You definitely wouldn't think guitars were wonderful if you were married to Ray! He'll sit there all day playing guitar, if he has the chance. It's even worse now he's got headphones, because I'm sure it sounds lovely to him, but all I'm getting is really crappy string sounds. I'm not getting the full effect. Even the boys say, 'Can't you get him to stop, Mum?'

When did you first hear about the birds and the bees?

SHERRIE: Nobody told me anything because I come from a time when sex wasn't discussed; you grew up and it just happened. I never knew what the birds and the bees were. I still don't! I simply don't understand what a bird does with a bee. It's beyond me, I'm afraid.

DENISE: My parents never gave me a birds and bees talk. I just had to find out about it for myself. I think I pretty much always knew about sex, but for ages I didn't know what a virgin was. I didn't know what the word meant and I was very embarrassed that I didn't.

Walking along the seafront with my friend Christine, when we were twelve or thirteen – and I'll remember this day forever – I said something like, 'If you had to describe what a virgin was, how would you, sort of, put it into words?' 'Well, somebody who hasn't had sex!' she said. 'Exactly! That's just how I would put it,' I said quickly. Since I didn't need to ask, 'What's sex?' I assume I did at least know the basics. It was just that I didn't know what the word 'virgin' meant.

SHERRIE: Have you ever given a birds and bees talk?

DENISE: No, I can't imagine it! I don't know who these children are who need a birds and bees talk.

COLEEN: Sex was one thing that was never discussed as I was growing up. I probably found out about relationships by watching my sisters. I saw them have boyfriends and cry – Linda used to cry on my shoulder about boys. Even as a young child, I thought, God, I'm never going to be like that! I would never cry like that over someone. I can't bear it! Through watching them, I learned the things I would and wouldn't do. I'd think, I must remember not to do that.

Sex was just unthinkable. I think that's why I was probably terrified of kissing boys. When I was twelve and thirteen, all my friends were off snogging, but I wasn't. A boy could put his arm round me or hold my hand, but if he tried to kiss me, I'd finish with him there and then. I was partly terrified, because I didn't know what to do. Practising on the back of your hand is all very well, I thought, but I'm sure it's not going to be like that when it actually happens!

LISA: I didn't know how to do the whole French kissing thing, but I suppose you just copy people, don't you?

COLEEN: Well, fear of my own ignorance held me back, but I also grew up in a family that believed only bad girls did that sort of thing. My mum never said anything outright, but I had the very clear impression that if you kissed lots of boys – and certainly, if you slept with boys – then you weren't a very nice girl. That was the Irish Catholic ethos. As a Catholic, you're practically born with guilt! I don't necessarily think that's a bad thing. That's where feminists would disapprove of me, because I don't want women to be like men. I can accept the idea of single men going out and having one-night stands every night of the week if they want to, but I'm still horrified when I find out that women do it.

LISA: I never had a birds and bees talk. Sex was never really discussed at home. Always lingering in the background was the idea that if you have sex, you can get pregnant and have a baby 'out of wedlock', which is exactly what happened to Mum. So sex was about secrets, about losing dignity, about giving something away that you shouldn't.

I still don't discuss sex with my mum. I don't know if other people my age do. I guess they would. When I got pregnant with Beau, I remember thinking, Now my mum knows I've had sex! I'm not only telling her that I'm pregnant; I'm telling her that I'm having sexual intercourse with my boyfriend at the same time.

For me the problem was that, in her experience, I think, sex was something that can have bad consequences. It's almost as if, in 'giving' it to somebody, you're allowing them to 'take advantage' of you in some way. I had to wrestle with this idea over the years to understand it, because for a long time I had this idea that you lost something in the process of having sex, when in fact you should be getting something back since you're both giving something to each other.

My bedroom was next to my nan and granddad's and I think I heard my granddad making a play for my nan one night. He growled loudly. 'Get off, you dirty b******!' she said. He growled again. 'Come on, Barbara, whoah!' he said. Well, my nan was called Rose! This sounds like a joke, but it's not. I think that was when I first thought that he was trying to get hold of my nan, but because she said, 'Get off, you dirty b******!' that probably cemented the idea in my head that it was dirty and that she wouldn't give it to him because he was drunk and she was punishing him.

LYNDA: Why did he call her Barbara if her name was Rose?

LISA: I don't know! There must have been a Barbara somewhere along the line, because whenever he got drunk or talked in his sleep, he'd always say, 'Ohhh, Barbara!' No one ever knew who she was and he took that secret to the grave with him.

LYNDA: How fascinating! That would definitely colour your idea of what sex was.

LISA: Yes, and probably not in a healthy way! What about you, Lynda? When did you start learning about all of this?

LYNDA: My school friends were well ahead of me and I think most of them had lost their virginity by the sixth form. I didn't even go to parties much, but one time I went to a party at Aylesbury Boys School and got stuck with a bloke on the bed upstairs. Lying on the bed, I thought, Oh my God, what now? To mask my confusion, I told him an endless stream of jokes. Every time he turned to touch me, I fell off the bed laughing. This went on a good half an hour, at which point he made his excuses and left. Apparently, word went round the boys school that there was absolutely no point in asking me out as I would talk all the way through the date. I was a subject of mockery, but it didn't bother me because I was so focused on my acting.

My whole attitude to relationships was based on being picked up and put down by my first love, Karel. Eventually, I became one of the lads, because I decided that it was better to be one of them, than not be with them at all. So we drank together at the pub and I paid my own way.

As time went on, I created a little life of my own at the Dark Lantern pub in Aylesbury, which I now realise was a den of iniquity in those days, frequented by all the local bad boys and people taking drugs. Of course, I didn't do drugs; I did half a cider. Often I'd say, 'Where's so and so?' 'Oh, he's "on holiday",' would come the reply, meaning he was in prison. I always just assumed he really was on holiday. Some of these men were much older than me; I was fifteen or sixteen and some of them were in their mid-twenties and mid-thirties, and yet there was an absolute understanding that I was safe with them. I heard all the dirty jokes and their not-always-very-nice comments about other women.

My parents were pretty clever and probably knew more than I did. One day Mum said, 'Dad says that at least we will never get burgled while you're friends with all these people!'

There was only one time that I had cause for concern, when

one of the locals gave me a lift home and tried to rape me. He had just come out of prison and must have been quite tipsy. He pinned me to the ground on the lawn outside the farmhouse but thankfully the dogs woke up and my dad opened the window and shouted out, so I got away. I was covered in green rot stains. 'What were you doing?' Dad asked. 'I fell over,' I said.

Realising that it could have been really unpleasant, I told the lads in the pub what had happened and he was told in no uncertain terms not to come near me again, which he didn't. I loved that camaraderie.

When I was accepted into drama school, I went to tell them all. 'Oh God, she'll turn into a right old slapper now,' they all laughed. 'I won't!' I protested. 'Give you ten minutes there and you'll be on your back with your legs in the air,' they teased. But I wasn't having any of it.

Although I desperately wanted to go to drama school, I didn't want to leave them behind and I often went back at weekends for the first eighteen months. Gradually I created the same kind of social circle in London. I was always out with the lads in the pub.

I might not have been the prettiest in the class, but I'm very extrovert with a good sense of humour, I have a passion and I am a very alive person, which are attractive qualities that can be mistaken for sexual openness. People thought I was very sexually liberated. Then it got confusing for me. How much should I conform to this image other people had of me? I still hadn't had sex and didn't know what I was talking about.

My best friend Nick and I were both virgins and were fascinated by sex. I went to live in Nick's flat with Nick and a

Portuguese guy called Carlos, who was a little bit older and a complete stud. He started going out with an American girl, Lena, and they had proper, grown-up sex. When they were at it, Nick and I would hide in the kitchen. We talked about them – and 'it' – endlessly!

After a while I discovered that the boys at drama school were putting bets on who was going to 'break me in'. I can't be doing with this! I thought, so I looked around and chose a boy in my year to lose my virginity to. It was also partly so that I could get a bit of experience, go home and seduce Karel.

Jay, the boy I chose, was very good looking. Everybody fancied him. Since I knew he wouldn't tell, I decided that he was going to be the one. We all got pissed as usual, Nick went off to bed and Jay and I did the deed in my room. Sadly, it didn't make much of an impact; I hardly knew it had happened! So that's it, is it? I thought. Well, I'm not that much bothered, really. I feel terrible about it now; Jay barely spoke to me again. Still, I don't regret it. When we've talked about it on *Loose Women*, some of the others have talked about how it happened with their first love and how it was the right time to do it. For me, it was actually about getting it out of the way.

LISA: It was the opposite for me! I snogged somebody and they touched my bum when I was fifteen or sixteen, but before then, nothing. It wasn't that I didn't want it, but I was incredibly choosy. My mother had drummed it into me that sex was such a special thing and if you were going to 'give' it to somebody, then you'd better make sure it was the right person. Since only Prince Andrew was good enough, in her eyes, I was sat in my

'One day, I'll be Mrs Essex . . .'

little flat in the Elephant and Castle, thinking, If only Prince Andrew knew I was here, he'd be over in a flash!

It's funny to think that my mum put me on a pedestal and I believed I had a right to be on it, which in my delusional way may well have saved me from a whole bunch of aggravation that I would otherwise have encountered.

LYNDA: Yes, it's strange how things work out!

LISA: So what happened after the first time, Lynda? Did you want to give it another try?

LYNDA: After that, if it was on offer at the end of the night, I did it, just because I could. It wasn't about looking for a boyfriend, it was about getting it out of the way and seeing whether I liked the person or not afterwards, because sex clouds everything.

I carried that on during the 1960s and it felt like real liberation. I chose who I slept with and I was the one who got out of the bed first the next day. I was never dumped. I was my own person, which meant equality to me then, mistakenly as it turns out. Equality to me was behaving like a man if I wanted to, instead of using what I was as a woman, to my best advantage.

My idea of equality meant that you had to ask a boy out. For somebody who didn't think highly of herself, I was remarkably forward. 'I suppose a f***'s out of the question?' I'd say. It was a way of shocking people, a way of getting in first, trying to be something I wasn't and overcoming the fear of disappointment. If I could just get all that stuff out of the way and they still liked me, that somehow made me all right. I don't know where that insecurity came from. Invariably they'd say yes, of course, because it was free and it was there, mate! My strategy always worked. I never got knocked back. No man is going to say no to a free session, so don't think it's because you are the most beautiful and desirable woman in the world. Instead you have to take hold of yourself and feel worthy and be aware of where proper emotions begin and that whole game ends.

I would say to a young woman now, 'Don't do what I did! You don't need to.' We have gone through the liberated period, the initial wonders of the pill and that idea of being free to have sex with whoever, whenever, wherever. We're all used to the idea that sex is much more open now and doesn't necessarily lead to pregnancy. So actually, it's better, not to use it as a prize, but to be aware that a really good relationship tends not to be about just dropping your knickers straight away. Sometimes that can happen, but in the main, you need to touch base with and flirt with that person, and know that person wants you passionately, before doing it.

The power of being brought up not to lose your virginity before you were married exerted a strong influence on me. I was a virgin until I was nineteen, so I was absolutely hanging on in there! Then, when I got to drama school, I became fed up with people assuming I wasn't a virgin. What's the point of holding back if everybody thinks I've already done it? I thought. It was like I shifted up a gear at that point and told my body that now I should want sex. But the teachings of my upbringing were still there, so I couldn't really relax and be a sexual person without drink. Inhibitions were the beginning of the alcohol problem for me. I had a lot of inhibitions that I found could easily be got rid of with a few drinks, something I had never realised before.

Young people are beautiful because they are young, but at the time you don't realise that and can't help worrying about not being cool. I never looked like I was supposed to. I didn't have a style. On the other hand it didn't matter, because I lived to act at drama school. For me, being with boys was about being accepted and being part of the drama school team. We were all in this together. We all went out together. I often used to say, 'We are all truly equal in the theatre, because we all pay for each other and we all earn the same money.'

There was the odd couple who were living together or having a relationship, which seemed slightly strange: how could they waste time with that when we were all in this group? It was a group effort. There's often an element of that when you look at young people now; they go round in groups. They might have sex but it is only an extension of the group, so it's never regarded as a real relationship. You are having a bit of sex, but the mother ship is always more important.

If I'm truly honest, I had lots of sex for years without it being good sex. I think that happens to lots of young women. Thank God I've since had good sex to compare it with! Of course, if you're lucky enough to have good sex initially, you're not going to accept rubbish sex and all that goes with it. Ah, it all seems so easy in hindsight.

DENISE: Yes, hindsight is a wonderful thing!

Is there such a thing as an ideal date?

DENISE: Are we talking hypothetically about a world in which I'm not married? I think most people's dream date would probably change every ten years or so. At one time my dream date would have involved copious amounts of alcohol and not very much food, then going out clubbing and ending up smooching in a drunken way to Lionel Richie at three in the morning. But that would be incredibly sad and probably an arrestable offence at my age! So now I'd just be happy with a quiet dinner. I'd still want Lionel Richie and a smooch, but probably somewhere slightly more private.

ANDREA: And Tim's ideal date?

DENISE: He'd probably want to go to his local pub with a three-foot woman who had a flat head. I think that's what a lot of men want really: she's in prime position for various things, as well as to balance your beer pot on!

COLEEN: Well, my ideal date would be very typical: meet in a lovely wine bar, meal, then maybe go to the pictures or the theatre. I wouldn't like to go clubbing. Preferably, it would be somewhere you could sit and chat. Obviously it's great if you're physically attracted to your date straight away, but you can sit and chat with somebody who initially hasn't made an impression and by the end of the night, if they've made you laugh, you're likely to be very attracted to them. So I think it's important to be somewhere you can get to know each other.

I think I'd rather he picked me up, because I would be terrified of walking into a wine bar and sitting on my own. If he didn't turn up to pick you up from home, no one need know, but if you walk out of a bar after waiting there alone, everyone's aware that you've been stood up. It's never happened to me, thank God.

SHERRIE: Or me! This sounds really tragic, but I don't even know what my ideal date would be. That kind of thing has gone off my radar; I've put it in a box and stored it away. It's disappeared from my life and I doubt it will ever come back. I couldn't even say to you, 'He would have to be like this,' or 'I'd like to do that.' All that is on my radar is my grandson, my daughter and my mother.

It would be really hard if somebody asked me out. I'd look at them as if they were an alien and say, 'Stop it! What are you doing?' I wouldn't believe that they really wanted to go out. Maybe things would be different if I met Robert Redford, but even he probably wouldn't live up to my expectations.

COLEEN: Come on Sherrie, don't think like that! There's the right person out there for you, you've just got to keep your eyes open so you don't miss him.

SHERRIE: Hmm, maybe!

LYNDA: Experience has taught me how important it is for you and your other half to have a similar outlook, culture, sense of humour and passion. It truly does matter. It makes it so easy to have a good time with somebody if they laugh at the same things. So I wouldn't really mind where I was with Mr Spain, although Venice would definitely be up there.

LISA: After going to New York with three Loose Women, I'd now like to have a night out in New York with Paul. I had such a blast. I wasn't sure if I was really going to enjoy it because I like my family life, being with my partner and having kids around. Being a *Sex and the City* girl just isn't me. Well, I absolutely loved it! I felt about 18 and liberated; there was a real solidarity with the girls. So my first thought for my ideal date was to go back with Paul to share some of that magic with him, but my suspicion is that maybe actually it should just be kept as a girl thing.

So perhaps it would be at the Four Seasons in Maui, where we went many moons ago and had the most memorable meal ever. We sat in the comfiest, most gorgeous big armchairs, overlooking the sunset on the ocean. We were childless and there was this feeling that we could get on a boat and go anywhere we wanted, without any preplanning.

We didn't have a lot of money then. We just spent all that we had left on the holiday on this meal. The maitre d' recommended a different wine with every course! We hadn't been together that long and as we sat there, looking at the sunset, I just knew that life was really, really good. So I'd like to go back and do that again!

How important is the venue on a first date?

CAROL: You don't want too much showing off, do you? I once started going out with a bloke and on our first date he offered to take me to this really posh London club called Annabel's. I thought, no! I might have to dance opposite him in a prom dress. I had a vision of him dancing in shoes and white socks and a blazer, because you have to wear a jacket in there. No, no, no, I thought.

'Let's just go to a restaurant,' I said. We went to quite a raucous restaurant in London where I knew it would be all right if you had too much to drink and fell out of the door. On a first date, you have to be really comfortable. Mark and I just went to local places, nothing impressive, nothing flash, and it works like that. You don't want to be impressed.

ANDREA: It can be something really simple, like having a bag of chips on a park bench, or a picnic. As long as you're in nice company, it doesn't really matter where you are.

CAROL: It depends where the chip shop is though, because the chips might be really cold by the time you get to the park bench! That wouldn't be very romantic, would it?

SHERRIE: I remember eventually going on my first date with a very gorgeous blond boy. I'm going to date myself now, because it was to see *Psycho* at the cinema – a really frightening film. We were on the back row and you know what that means! It's snogging time! I had a big thing of popcorn. I was eating my popcorn and he had his arm around me and I thought, any minute now! Then came the bit in the shower with the scary music and the shower curtain and suddenly my popcorn flew up in the air, showered the woman in front and got stuck all over her bouffant hair! I didn't see the rest of the film because I spent my time trying to pick it all out without her noticing! It was the funniest thing. I never saw him again!

What's the most disastrous thing
that could happen on a date?

DENISE: Farting would not be great. In fact, it would be absolutely horrendous. Silence and cutlery-clinking would also be terrible. I have overcompensated for that in the past, because my nightmare in any social situation is to hear nothing but the clink-clink that means nobody has anything to say.

Also, I would have to make my excuses and leave if somebody ate with their mouth open. I can't bear noisy eating and stuff like that. And a man not performing very well in bed at the end of the date would be a great disappointment.

SHERRIE: Have you ever had a really disastrous date?

DENISE: Actually, I think I've always made the most of them!

COLEEN: Not fancying him is pretty disastrous. After my marriage to Shane, I went on a date where I knew straight away that although I really liked the guy, I didn't fancy him. Then, an hour into the date, he said, 'So how do you think I could get into the business?' Oh no! I thought, now he's asking me for career advice as well! All night I was thinking, Oh God, he's going to try and kiss me! But I knew that there was never going to be anything romantic between us, so I had to think of a way to avoid him trying to kiss me.

One of my sisters was looking after my son for the night. I phoned her about 10p.m. and said, 'I'm going to come and pick him up.' As my date was driving me home, I said, 'Can we stop and pick my son up? He needs to come home with me because he's not feeling very well.' I knew he wouldn't go in for a kiss in front of my son.

SHERRIE: When I was eighteen, I had a sort-of date with Steve McQueen. He came to RADA to give a talk and I was chosen to take him around on a red London bus. It was the date to end all dates! Later, he took me to a beautiful restaurant called the Poissonnerie. Unfortunately I didn't realise that 'poisson' means fish – and I'm allergic to fish. 'I'll order,' he said. I was so nervous that I couldn't speak; in fact, I hardly spoke all day. The waiter put a plate of seafood in front of me and I politely ate the lot. But then I projectile vomited all over Steve McQueen! I actually thought I was going to be Mrs Steve McQueen until that happened.

LISA: Oh no, Sherrie, poor you! I have to be honest and say that I've never really done dating. But I was once picked up by my first love in a car, so maybe that counts, although he was a thief and he'd probably nicked it.

I had borrowed my friend's white leather skirt with fringing. It was a really rude skirt; it only just covered my vitals before the fringing started. So whenever I moved or danced around, it only just covered my modesty! At one point, I deliberately leaned forward to give him a flash of my bum, which was a bit naughty of me.

He took me to a nightclub in Battersea called Bennetts. I'll never forget it because it had fish under the glass dance floor! Afterwards, we went back to his flat and I left my make-up bag there. Any excuse to go back! Now I knew where he lived, I was a bit of a stalker around him.

I rang him and rang him, but he didn't call me back for a

week. So I pretended to take our dog for a walk and found my way to where he lived. I knocked at the door and he opened it in a dressing gown, looking really flustered. Unfortunately, the girl he had been with for years and years had moved back in! I was absolutely devastated.

SHERRIE: You poor thing! It sounds like it was good fun until then, though.

LISA: Yes, it was a proper grown-up nightclub and the kind of place that only local gangsters could get you into.

COLEEN: Have you had any other dating disasters, Sherrie?

SHERRIE: How did you know? About five years ago, I went for dinner with a man. This was my one and only attempt at going on a date after my marriage broke up. He was a very nice man, tall and good looking, with money and a good job. Everybody said, 'You'll like him.'

I was staying at a friend's in Surrey; she engineered the whole thing. 'You never go out,' she said. 'You must give it a try.' I looked at a picture of him and said, 'OK, he's not ugly. All right. I'll go out with him.' But as I was getting ready, I kept thinking, I don't want to do this. And the more I thought about it, the sulkier I became, like a child. Stop doing that! I told myself. It's not fair. But by now I was really resentful that I was even going out of the door.

He arrived in a very nice car and he was beautifully dressed. 'He has a lovely car!' my friend said encouragingly. 'I know, I can see,' I said. As I got in the car, I was thinking, you know, he is quite a nice man! We started to chat and he explained what he did; I think he worked for a manufacturing company, but I can't really remember.

He was very polite when we arrived at the restaurant and pulled my chair out to let me sit down. Lovely manners! I thought. Then, disaster struck . . .

'What would you like to drink?' he asked, adding, 'Obviously, I'm driving.'

'OK . . .' I said.

'Do you just want a glass of wine?' he went on.

'No, we may as well have a bottle of wine,' I said, even though I can't drink more than two glasses.

'Well, I'm driving . . .' he said.

'Yeah,' I said, deliberately not taking the hint.

'Oh, right, yes, sorry, we will have a bottle of wine,' he said, 'We can always cork it and take it home.'

'We won't need to,' I said. I was being really antagonistic; I don't know why.

When the bottle of wine arrived, he insisted on pouring it. 'No, let me,' he said.

I was becoming really irritated now. He poured the wine, but only half a glass. Now he's not going to let me drink this wine because he can't have any! I thought. His attitude struck me as rather selfish. As a result, when he started to talk, I reacted negatively to everything he said. So when he mentioned that he was thinking of buying a place in Spain, I said, 'I don't like Spain.' Not that he was asking me to go, or anything!

'I thought you liked Spain,' he said. 'You lived there, after all.'

'That was when I was with my ex-husband,' I said with a scowl.

'Right,' he said.

I was very conscious of what I was doing and I was getting really upset with myself, but I couldn't help it. 'Would you like some more wine?' he asked a little later.

'Yes!' I said, reaching quickly for the bottle and pouring myself a whole glass.

'Right, shall we cork the rest?'

'No!'

'Do you want to drink it all?'

'Yes!'

It was just the most ridiculous thing. I drank the whole bottle deliberately, for no other reason than that he didn't want me to drink it. Of course, after drinking nearly a whole bottle of wine as if it were Ribena, I felt awful: dizzy, uncoordinated and slightly sick. 'Would you like anything else?' he asked politely. He was so sweet and so nice.

'Yes, I'll have another glass of red wine,' I said defiantly.

'Sorry?'

'I will have another glass of red wine, please.' He duly ordered me another. After that, I was a little bit wobbly when I got up from the table. 'I think you've had a bit too much to drink,' he said, stating the obvious.

Well, that was it. 'Don't tell me how much is too much!' I snapped. 'You can't tell me about red wine.'

'I'm sorry, I was just saying . . .'

'I'm not drunk!' I insisted, although I was staggering all over the restaurant. To make things worse, on the way out I lurched down the stairs and tripped at the bottom. Now I looked stupid. He put his arm out to steady me. 'Don't help me!' I said.

Feeling angry and sick, I got in the car and he drove me back to my friend's house. Well – and this is the worst part of all – he walked me to the door and tried to kiss me goodnight. 'I don't think so!' I said, pushing him aside. 'Stand back!'

LISA: Crikey Sherrie!

SHERRIE: When I got into the house, my friend said, 'Oh my God. What happened to you?' That night I was sick and I was sick the next day. It was awful. 'Why did you do this?' she asked. The poor man phoned her boyfriend and said about me, 'She's the strangest girl. I'm not sure I really want to see her again! I think you should tell her that she drinks too much. She's definitely got a drink problem.'

He has since texted me, 'How are you?

'I'm OK. Not in rehab,' I replied, still being defensive.

The stupid thing is that if he had just said, 'What do you fancy?' I would probably have asked for water. Or I'd have said, 'Since you're driving, I'll just have a glass of wine.' But because he was virtually telling me that I didn't want more than a glass because he wasn't having any, I became defensive. It makes me go cold to remember it, because I feel so embarrassed.

In fact, I shouldn't have gone out with him in the first place, because I wasn't open to being on a date. In that case, don't do it; that's the way I feel now. Don't spoil your evening, and don't spoil someone else's evening either. I'd rather just say no. So that's what I mean when I say it's no longer on my radar. I don't experience a frisson with anyone I meet. I'm probably closed to it, but I can't recall the last time I thought, Wow, I'd like to get to know him. I have no interest whatsoever. It's sad and it can be lonely, but I'm OK.

LISA: Don't be lonely Sherrie – we love you!

What are the dos and don'ts of dating?

DENISE: I would never, ever, ever read a dating guide if I were single. I hate those types of books: 'How To Seduce Men' and 'How To Date'. Oh God, anybody who has to use a manual might as well just give up!

LISA: Don't go looking for love. Men can smell it when women are looking for love and commitment. Just try and have as much fun as you can on the way. I know that it's easier said than done, but get on with your life. Hopefully a by-product of that will be that you'll meet someone who will be watching you having a good time who thinks, she looks like a bloody good laugh! I might go and talk to her.

How to flirt . . .

ANDREA: Jane, remind me of your five-point guide to flirting?

JANE: No, Andrea, not again!

ANDREA: Please? Some people may not know about it . . .

JANE: But it's all so long ago! Since I met Ed, I've forgotten all about it. But OK, here goes:

1. Spot someone you like, and if he likes you back, he will hold your gaze for more than five seconds.
2. Then, when you see that he is holding your gaze, give him

'What first attracted me to her? Well . . .
it would have to have been her personality . . .'

a smile. But not a fake one, a real one, because a smile is the most inviting thing for a man. (Oooh, hark at me, as if I know what I'm doing!)

3. The smile is usually the invite. If he approaches you, which he will if there's interest from both parties, be interested in what he has to say about his life. It's not all about you.

4. From then on, it's all in the eyes. You know they say that the eyes are the windows to your soul? Well, they are, and you can usually tell everything from them.

5. Start playing with your hair. That's always a dead giveaway. If he starts playing with his hair as well, you know you're in.

Do you believe in the concept of leagues when it comes to looks? Can someone be 'out of your league'?

JANE: I would like to think that it doesn't matter, but I think it really does. I mean, I would never, ever go after somebody like David Beckham . . .

ANDREA: Because he's married!

JANE: Well, yes, but really because I know he's out of my league. You would go for a one-night stand with somebody like that, but you know you couldn't carry it on. Well, I personally couldn't. When I first met my partner, Ed, he was a big pop star and I was a barmaid. At the time, I just knew that I would not be able to keep up with his rock and roll lifestyle. So I left and let him get on with his life for a while. I'm glad that we've come back together now, but he was way out of my league in the early days.

ANDREA: Was that to do with his lifestyle, or did you think he was too good looking for you?

JANE: A bit of both. He was absolutely beautiful. He's lovely now, but he was stunningly beautiful and I thought, I can't compete with that. The girls used to throw themselves at him – and the boys, I have to say. He used to wear little Lycra shorts and a tie! He just wears the tie now!

CAROL: I used to think that everybody was out of my league – and I still do, actually. I've never really chatted anybody up and if anyone chats me up or expresses an interest, I'm like, Really? Now I'm all right, because I've got Mark. Some people might look at him and think, he's way out of her league. Because he's young and handsome and fit and gorgeous – ooh!

LYNDA: You see, I think you really look similar. You're absolutely suited and it's a perfect coupling. You are a very attractive couple.

CAROL: We do look a bit alike, yes.

LYNDA: I think this idea of leagues is a bit silly really, because actually beauty really is in the eye of the beholder. Everybody finds their partner and it might be Mr Average or it might be Mr Muscle. So this is a very superficial way of looking at things.

CAROL: It probably is, but when I was younger, it didn't matter how good looking or rich they were, I would go for anything. Honestly, I would!

ANDREA: You're making all your past boyfriends feel very special!

CAROL: No, but if I wanted someone, I would go after them and get them. Not all the time, obviously, but then as I got older, I started to think, Oh, no, out of my league!

ANDREA: Do you think it's to do with confidence, rather than looks or chemistry? Because Steve is the most confident man I've ever met: he can bowl into a room, saying, 'All right, darling?' He can chat to anyone. It doesn't matter if it's the Prime Minister or someone emptying the bins: he will talk to everyone in the same way and like everyone the same. Most people like him for that. When I met him, that's what I liked about him. It wasn't how he looked or anything.

LYNDA: He's not got a league in mind, has he? That's lovely. I remember going out for a bit with a director who was incredibly intelligent, and I thought, I couldn't keep this up for long; I'd have to start doing the crossword!

CAROL: There's incompatibility, isn't there? The 'out of my league' thing is in the mind, whereas you can look at certain people and think, there is absolutely no way, because you'd have nothing in common with them.

LYNDA: You long to reassure somebody young who is led astray by the idea that if you're not beautiful, you're not worthy. Actually, the last person you want to go out with is someone who thinks they're beautiful and that everybody else should be beautiful around them. They're usually very boring and have some terrible problem!

Does dating a younger man keep you youthful?

ANDREA: According to some new research by a dating website, dating a younger man can keep you young. In fact, they reckon it can knock off four years from a woman's age. This is all because it will encourage you to do more outdoor activities (wink wink), mix with people with youthful hobbies, dress differently and try new things. So how old are you, Carol McGiffin?

CAROL: All those things are absolutely true. Before I met Mark, I was going to move to Paris and I was a little bit tired of my surroundings. Not bored, but I'd just had enough and I thought, I've got to shake things up; I need some excitement; I need an adventure. Then Mark came along and everything that I'd found I wasn't enjoying anymore, like where I live and listening to certain music and things like that, suddenly became enjoyable again.

I don't want to compare it to having children, because he's not a child, but it is like seeing everything through new eyes, like you would do if you had kids and they were growing up. So it does keep you young, because you have to make more effort and that's a fact. I've said before that I was quite looking forward to wearing skirts with elasticated waists and just sitting around, not brushing my hair. Well, sometimes I don't brush my hair. But then you go and get a gorgeous young man . . .

ANDREA: But the research says that it will encourage you to do more outdoor activities. Have you?

CAROL: Well, you know . . . we sometimes walk around Camden Town.

'Rebecca, your roses are in a wonderful condition . . . and I can think of something else that's looking pretty good too . . . !'

ANDREA: OK, mix with people with youthful hobbies?

LISA: Skateboarding?

CAROL: No, not skateboarding, but going to the pub – is that a youthful hobby?

ANDREA: That's ageless. And dress differently?

CAROL: I've always dressed quite young for my age and I have been accused of being a bit mutton dressed as lamb.

SHERRIE: You did find the bleach. That's the only thing.

CAROL: No, I dyed my hair before Mark came along. It's true that there are loads of wonderful things about going out with a younger guy, but at the same time, it is hard to keep up.

ANDREA: Sherrie, all those things sound very exciting. Don't you fancy that?

SHERRIE: Well, a few years ago, I did meet a younger man. He was very much younger. The thing is, I couldn't do it because, think about it – when you can't see in the dark . . . and there was no way I was going to take any clothes off in the light.

CAROL: That's the best bit about being with a younger man.

SHERRIE: No, no no! You've got to look in the mirror and you don't want them looking at that, do you?

CAROL: But maybe he likes it! Not maybe – if he got that far, he would!

LISA: But it's hard to keep it up.

CAROL: What?

LISA: Looking young and making sure you always look your best. Paul's five years younger than me and that's quite a difference.

SHERRIE: You have to remember that the memories are very different, as well. My memories would be very different to this boy's, so you can't talk about certain things. You do say that sometimes, Carol.

CAROL: Absolutely. His Dr Who is David Tennant and mine was Jon Pertwee.

SHERRIE: Your children's TV was *Wooden Tops* and his is . . .

CAROL: CBeebies! No, it's not, I'm joking!

LISA: Do you not get fed up with knowing more than your partner? Because you do just know more stuff when you're older!

CAROL: No, he knows lots of things that I don't know.

LISA: Like what?

CAROL: Things, you know! Things and stuff!

ANDREA: That's not to do with age. That's to do with being a woman and being a man!

CAROL: What do you do to keep up with Paul?

LISA: Well, I was 33 when I met him and he was 28, and that felt like quite a big gap, but now we're both forty-la-la, there's no difference.

CAROL: You've been together for ages, as well.

LISA: Yes, we've been together for ages and he's always had really bad eyesight. Yes!

CAROL: That's so handy! So has Mark. He can't see a thing!

LISA: In the morning: blind as a bat! It's fabulous. I've got no make-up on and he says, 'Cor, you're lovely.' I'm thinking, come on!

CAROL: Don't go and put your contact lenses in yet! Keep them out for another hour.

SHERRIE: Has he got a brother that has just as bad eyesight?

When did you realise you had found The One, and were your friends in agreement with you?

COLEEN: Actually, my friends and family worried a lot when I met Ray.

KATE: Really?

COLEEN: They were worried because of everything I'd been through and they were worried that it wasn't going to last. Of course, it all happened so fast. I mean, everything! Met in July, pregnant by September!

KATE: Was it really that quick?

COLEEN: You know, my friends were worried, but I knew within 48 hours that he was The One. I was older and I'd been through so much in my life already, so it wasn't a case of, Oh, here's someone interesting; I'm just going to settle for anyone. We both just absolutely clicked. We made each other laugh and we had loads in common.

Actually, there was also loads that we didn't have in common, which made it more interesting, because it meant that we would have something to discuss. So I knew he was The One immediately and my friends have gradually realised over the last ten years that I'm not messing about. I think they're taking me seriously now!

KATE: It's easy to write off a relationship that starts in haste, isn't it? But I suppose there are exceptions to the rule and you are certainly that, Coleen.

JANE: Actually, when I first met my other half, Sue, my backing singer, knew straight away – and so did you, Coleen.

COLEEN: I did, straight away. I think your friends can pick up on it. I knew, because you changed instantly.

JANE: Did I?

COLEEN: You became all giggly and girly. You weren't saying, 'I'd rather have a cup of tea,' anymore! You were asking, 'What shall I wear?' And just that smile, which you've still got, which is quite sickening really . . .

KATE: You are quite male in your attitude, aren't you? Much like Carol.

JANE: Yes.

KATE: And you've both been softened by these men that have found their ways into your lives. Look, she's smiling again!

JANE: I'm feeling right giddy, because he's coming home in two weeks. I can't wait to . . . you know . . . say, 'How's your tour been?'

KATE: I bet you'll be saying a few other things besides!

Do men and women want different things from a relationship?

COLEEN: Men and women are so different in what they want. I need much more emotional reassurance than Ray does. Sometimes I say to him, 'I just need a hug!'

'What's up with you?' he'll say. 'Why are you being moody?'

'I just need a hug!'

'What for?'

That's the only bit where we're not on the same page! He's definitely not a hearts and flowers man and when he is romantic, which isn't very often, it stands out a mile. It's lovely then, because it's a massive gesture. But if he felt I was expecting it the whole time, he would never do it.

I'm over-romantic. I say, 'Shall we cuddle and watch telly?'

'Shall we just watch telly?' he'll say. 'Why do you need to lie in my space?'

'Well, it would be romantic!'

'No, it's not romantic, it's ridiculous. You'll just make me hot.'

We laugh about it, but if I'm being a bit insecure and feel I need a reassuring hug, he doesn't get it. 'If you want hearts and flowers every day, you're with the wrong man,' he says.

'I don't want that! But now and again I need a hug.'

He finds it really hard. Having said that, if I hold his hand on the sofa or walking down the street, he won't pull it away. But he won't initiate it – it always has to be me – and sometimes that annoys me, because I think, God, if I didn't do it, I don't think we'd ever touch.

I think it might be to do with his upbringing. He's very close to his mum and dad; they love each other very much, but they weren't tactile. He can't remember getting a hug from his mum or dad and yet he adores them. On the other hand, my mum gave me a million hugs. She hugged me whenever I was hurt or crying, and often she just grabbed me and hugged me, which is something I do with my kids all the time.

Ray's mum is eighty-five and he takes her shopping every week. When he says goodbye to her, he gives her a kiss on the cheek. 'Do you not think I want to wrap my arms around her and give her the biggest hug?' he says. 'But I can't, because I think she would be uncomfortable and I would probably be uncomfortable too.' So I think that's the way he's grown up.

After ten years, I've noticed that he is more tactile than he was when we first met. He's very tactile with the boys and with Ciara. He gives the boys hugs when they're going out and they will with him. But the romance thing is slightly different.

At the same time, he's the first guy I've been with where I've felt 100 per cent sure that he's in my corner. If anybody hurts me or is horrible to me, he wants to kill them. When the press print something nasty or untrue about me, I'm less sensitive than I used to be. 'It doesn't matter,' I'll say to Ray. 'You know what the press are like.' But he gets very defensive. 'They've no right to say that about you!' That means a lot to me, I think it's lovely.

The first time around, I was married to somebody who was ultra romantic, who left notes every time he went to the toilet, let alone when he went to the shop! He gave me flowers and beautiful cards day to day. He was very tactile and wouldn't let me sit two inches away from him on the couch. But he was behaving in the same way to a million other girls behind my back, so who's to say which is the right and which the wrong way?

DENISE: Well, I think that if we're talking about conventional women, then there is no doubt that they are more interested in the emotional investment that a man is going to put into a relationship. I have many friends who would never be able to sleep with somebody until there was some emotional connection. Obviously, I have always been very open about the fact that it wasn't always the same for me.

However, if I were single now, at my age, my views would probably be very different to how they were when I was younger, before I was married. I'd probably be looking for a life partner, so I wouldn't be as gung ho about it all. That might partly be in self-protection, because men certainly wouldn't be as gung ho about having a one night stand with me as maybe they were years ago.

LYNDA: Don't be so sure! Younger men are probably looking for the superficially pretty person because on some level, even if it's sub-conscious, they want you to breed. But youth being as fickle as it is, the beauty of the day is about what is trendy. It is always media led.

I don't know how it happened, but nowadays there are so many young women who are motivated by money. I look at my sons and I feel sorry for them. If you haven't got money, if you're not famous or in the right group or the leading macho stud, these women pass you over.

Did I burn my bra so that a girl can rely on a footballer to support her? No, I went out and got my own money and won my independence. These girls seem to expect to live off a man and be given everything without even treating him with any respect or kindness. I mean, if you are going to live off a man, the least you can do is sometimes pander to his needs!

LISA: I wouldn't know. Like you, I've always been fiercely independent and earned my own money.

Maybe at the beginning of a relationship you're looking for different things, but as you get to know each other and get closer, the glue that keeps you together is wanting the same things. If one of you wants kids and one of you doesn't, for instance, that's a big stumbling block.

I've never gone out with anyone for money. Unfortunately, I've never been smart enough! I've fallen for the feather cut and for the thief with the cheeky smile and a good line in spiel, but I've never looked for money. I've always liked nice things, though, and I've worked hard and ended up with everything I've ever wanted materially.

LYNDA: Good for you! That's a real achievement. But when it comes to men, I do think they ultimately want a woman in the kitchen and a whore in bed. If you can get that right, you've cracked it.

SHERRIE: Really? I don't know what men look for in a woman. I could never work out what men want. Most of my male friends are gay. I love them because they don't need, want or expect anything from me, except friendship. So that makes my life easy.

Is a needy man a turn off?

JANE: Let's be honest, here: a man obviously needs confirmation that you care about him, just as a woman needs it. We've all thought, I wonder if he loves me? Men do exactly the same thing. Sometimes we get so caught up in our days and there's so much going on that we don't give them reassurance. Especially when you have babies and family, they're really far down the list. So a needy man sometimes just needs a little bit of reassurance that you're thinking about him.

CAROL: I bet you do that.

JANE: I do! In the past, I've not reassured partners and it's a very bad thing. Now I'm older, I do reassure my partner and the people around me and I reassure my mother every day that I love her very much. We should all think a little bit more about that. Everybody wants to be needed.

CAROL: Yes, but needy is draining, though! I don't want to have to reassure someone all the time.

JANE: Not all the time; just now and again.

CAROL: No, I don't want needy. I think that's why I don't have children, because they are endlessly needy. I don't want to be needed all the time; it would wear me out. With a bloke, it would drive me bananas! I'd constantly be saying, 'No, get off me!'

KATE: I've been with men who seek constant reassurance and it's the biggest turn-off ever. I find it really claustrophobic.

CAROL: It's the same as being insecure!

KATE: Yes, it's very unsexy. But I think there's a difference between wanting someone and needing them. I've always said to Darren, 'I don't need you, but I really want you.' I make sure that he feels wanted, but needed?

ZOE: Don't you need a cuddle?

KATE: No, I *want* a cuddle.

ZOE: Don't you need affection?

KATE: No, I *want* affection.

ZOE: They're very close, needing and wanting.

KATE: I need air, food and water; those are the things I need, if I'm being blunt about it. I want him to know that I love him, but I don't *need* him to know that, because the way that we are with each other tells him that, anyway.

JANE: I'm very much in control; I control everything in my life. That's the type of person I am. I couldn't have a man who was very independent, who didn't need me. Because I haven't got children, I nurture in another way.

ZOE: When I was married, my ex-husband wasn't needy, but at

the same time he was a little bit insecure. It's all a bit confusing for me: I want to be wanted and, in a tiny way, I'd like to be needed. Because I'm nurturing and I like to give, I would want that back.

CAROL: That kind of implies dependence and you don't want someone to be dependent on you. The only thing I ever need, really, is a glass of wine.

KATE: Oh yes, I left that off my list!

Chapter 3

Image and sexuality

LIFE BETWEEN THE SHEETS AND IN FRONT OF THE MIRROR

It's interesting to speculate about what life would be like if you were a man, and even more interesting to imagine being a man in bed! Would you be a considerate lover, a wimp or a stallion? Can you really say that you wouldn't like to try it, just the once?

Sex is an endlessly fascinating, multi-faceted subject. (Well, it is if you're a woman! Men don't seem to be so driven to analyse it in the kind of detail that we do, unless they're secretly doing it behind our backs. What *do* they talk about at the pub, anyway?) So does seduction means something different to each of the sexes and is there such a thing as bed etiquette? Much is made of sexual fantasies, but are they really a good thing?

We're divided as to whether sex really is so different for men and women: perhaps the idea of separating love and sex isn't just a male thing, because at least two of us have found that we can do it! But for the rest of us, it's definitely important to seek an emotional connection when it comes to the physical side of a relationship, and maybe that's the case for some men as well.

Sometimes our attitude to sex can be influenced by what we

look like, especially when we haven't got any clothes on. Argh! But, you know, perhaps men aren't quite so bothered about our flaws as we are, partly because they're too busy worrying about their own. And maybe they don't actually expect us to be perfect. So don't feel bad as you reach for that extra biscuit. Just tell yourself it's true that they'd rather have something to grab hold of – because it is! That's something we all agree on here at *Loose Women*: stick thin is for insects only!

If you were a man for a day, what would you do?

COLEEN: If I were a man for a day, I would probably sleep with a lot of people, to get my head round the idea that men can separate sex from emotions and love. Apparently, it's not about loving your girlfriend less: it's there, on a plate, and it's sex. I'd like to experience that. I'd also like to know what it feels like when your bits are on the outside.

LYNDA: So are you jealous of women who can do that, then?

COLEEN: No, but I'd like to know whether men are winding me up about it. Are they using it as an excuse to get away with it, by saying, 'It's different for men.' Or is it a fact? I actually believe that it's a fact, because I've seen some of the women that my male friends have pulled at the end of the night and I've thought, it must be to do with sex and nothing else!

Also, you know how highly sexed men are, because they wake up with it in the morning. Whereas I don't open my eyes and think, Oh yeah, I need sex now . . . It's more like, I need a cup of tea . . . So it must be weird to wake up with a hard-on.

I'd like to go out with a group of lads and hear what they really talk about. I've always suspected it's all football, jokes and drink and apparently that's exactly right. From what I'm told, they don't discuss personal issues. I've asked my husband, sons, exes, brothers and friends. If you have a row at home, they'll go out and say, 'Wife's been a pain in the ass. Get us a beer, will you?' And their mates will say, 'Do you want to talk about it?' And the answer's, 'Nah.' Whereas a woman would say, 'Let me tell you what's happened tonight!' She'd go through the whole thing and listen to her friends' and sisters' advice.

You know, I've never thought that I'd like to be a man for a day. Not even for one minute! Yet I absolutely adore men and I would hate to be without them.

SHERRIE: Since we live in a male-dominated world, if I were a man for a day, I think I'd want to run a big company like ITV, or be Prime Minister, just to see how it feels to be so powerful. I know it isn't as glamorous as it looks and it must be pretty frightening, because you have so many people to answer to. But I'd like to try it anyway. I'd like to say, 'Come on, let's sort you all out.' It would be interesting to see what could be done, to address the state the country is in. Why and how did it get to this point? It can't have happened without people floundering around, so there's a temptation to think, if I could have just been there to get a grip, things would be different, although I know the reality would be much more complex than that.

I think it's totally wrong to assume that women will get

stressy and emotional about making big, important decisions. Women can absolutely differentiate between emotion and business, when they need to. I know I can. Whereas men have one side, I think women have two.

Like Coleen though, what I'd like to know is what men talk about in the pub. We know what girls talk about, because that's *Loose Women*. But I often say to men, 'What do you actually talk about? Do you ever talk about your feelings or sex?' And they say, 'No, we talk about football and golf.' You know something? I think that really is all they talk about! There's the occasional, 'Cor, look at that. I wouldn't mind that,' and all that rubbish, when an attractive woman comes into the room. But I do wonder about the actual conversations they have. Can they really be so straightforward?

LYNDA: If I were a man for a day, I'd like to get in a really fast car and drive it at top speed. I would also like to pull. I'd go to a pub or a bar where I liked the atmosphere and the people, and I'd see what happened next. If I made an obvious pull, I would follow it through. In the evening, I would back off and see if I could meet somebody who wasn't quite such an obvious pull, someone I'd make a real connection with. But if I'd met somebody at lunchtime and made that connection, and if I thought, this could be really good, I would then want to spend the rest of the day and the night with that person to see where it went. I don't necessarily mean going to bed.

My first thought is that I'd feel I was much more in control of that situation as a man than as a woman. I could see where I could lead things by buying her lunch and then watch how far she would go to keep the connection going. But the trouble is, I can't imagine it would make a difference to me whether I was a man or a woman in that situation. I'd probably behave in exactly the same way.

Let's leave it at the fast car! Oh, and if I were a man I'd like to go to a gym and hang out with a load of men in a shower or a steam room to see what they said. Or spend an evening with a group of men at the pub, so that I could hear their every comment and absolutely nail them down.

LISA: If I were a young man, I'd go out on the pull with a bunch of women who were also out on the pull. Who would I connect with, and why? That would fascinate me.

I'd also like to try being a man with a pregnant partner, to see whether they feel anything at all when you're pregnant. They read the books and make the right noises and say the right things, but I don't believe that anything at all is going on in their body or mind. It's all going on with you and they have to pretend to go along with it, but I'd like to know if anything does change in their world during pregnancy and childbirth. They have to play the role of a father-to-be, but nothing's happening to them, except that their girlfriend or wife has now got really fat and unbearable to live with! Do they really love the fact that you're having their child?

LYNDA: Oh yes, I'd love to find out about that too!

Would you like to try being a man in bed?

SHERRIE: No, is the answer to that!

DENISE: I would love to see what it feels like to not have to think about things when you are doing it! To just be taken over by desire. We women have to put a little bit more cerebral input into things to get ourselves in the mood and stay there, but they don't. I'd love to experience my brain being taken over! There can't be many women who wouldn't like to try it. And I think I've witnessed enough to have learnt from the best!

LYNDA: I think I would be a good lover as a man because I know that as a woman, what turns me on is being made to think I am the most incredible person. The people who are interesting and good at sex are the ones who make you feel you are the most important thing in their life. I don't know if I'm allowed to say this, but a woman once told me that she had been to bed with Jack Nicholson. Obviously, I asked her what he was like. 'You think you are the only woman in his life for those two hours,' she told me. 'It is incredible.'

A great lover whisks you away. He may have no intention of ever seeing you again, but he makes you feel like you have had a strong emotional connection. OK, he knows how to move you into this position or that one, and that's terrific, but most women have to feel an emotional connection of some kind. If he is interested and it's all about you, you'll do anything, because he makes you feel you are so beautiful and perfect. Even if you think it's ridiculous on an

'Best to get these things out of the way first, don't you agree?'
said Natalie, as she 'sized' up her blind date

intellectual level, it doesn't matter. You are there; nobody else is.

For some men, it's all about trying to make you have an orgasm. Instead of doing it because you are so perfect to make love to, they will bring out all their tricks, and if you don't have an orgasm, there can be some resentment from them. That's not good news. It is about giving, really. I didn't have orgasms for years, because I wasn't giving anything of myself to the men I was going bed with. I was keeping it all inside me.

Whether it's a one night stand or thirty years of marriage, I think what defines being good in bed is when both of you are both dedicated to that moment together. All you are thinking about is that person in front of you.

LISA: I would like to try being a man in bed, because I can't imagine why it's such an amazing feeling for them. It sounds really crude, but it's a bit like putting your hand in someone's stomach during an operation, isn't it? What feels nice about that? Rubbing your toilet part around someone's innards? I don't get that! All that jelly organ stuff – doesn't it just feel like someone's intestines? I don't understand why it gives them the sensation that it gives them. I would really like to know.

I think I'd be a good lover, but I'd probably be quite competitive and try to be a bit too much of a stallion!

How would your partner cope if he became a woman for a day?

COLEEN: If Ray became a woman? I think he'd love the fact that there were two lesbians in the bed – me and him! That would be his dream come true.

LISA: I think Paul would be an amazing woman. In fact, I think he'd cope better than me!

DENISE: Tim is going off to play a transvestite in *Benidorm*, so he will be a woman for more than a day. He is very good at being my wife when I am away, so it wouldn't be a huge change for him. He'd go to the supermarket and do the tea like he does normally.

SHERRIE: Do you know something? I haven't got a clue about the answer to this one! I didn't know my ex all that well, even after twenty-six years. That was the problem. How would he cope with being a woman for a day? He would probably find it hysterical. He always thought that women made a meal of things and were too emotional, when in fact they did nothing all day. 'A woman for a day?' he'd say. 'What am I going to do? Sit at home and do nothing? Is that what you mean? You don't do anything anyway.' I'd be thinking, oh yes, that's what we do. We do nothing. Grrrr!

In fact, I did everything. I painted, gardened, cooked, ironed, washed, vacuumed, everything. Even when I was in *Coronation Street*, I would go out to work at 6a.m., come back at 7p.m. and still cook, clean and wash. I sound like a martyr, but I'm not. I just got on and did it. My dad didn't come with me when we moved to Manchester, unfortunately!

I always say to my daughter, 'Don't cook, clean, iron, wash, paint, no, because that's what I did for twenty-six years. Don't have the life that I had.' I don't know why I say it to her really, because her situation is very different, especially since she has a happy relationship. She is fantastic though; she can do everything. Her house is always beautiful and neat and her garden is like something out of a magazine.

DENISE: Would she like to come and live with me?

Should the man take the lead in bed?

LISA: No, I think men love it when you take the initiative. It's often better if women take the lead.

LYNDA: I reckon a lot of women think that the man is supposed to do everything in bed. But why do we assume that he is going to be any better at it or know any more about it? I sometimes wonder whether the majority of people don't get beyond the missionary position, because nobody likes to suggest anything else. A man might not like to suggest to his wife, who is the adoring mother of his children, that perhaps she might like to bend over the kitchen table. Because perhaps the woman would think, why are you treating me without respect?

You should be able to sit down with your loved one and say, 'I want to be the best at everything with you. If you know more than me, please teach me. If I happen to know some-thing that, say, I've read in a book, I'll tell you about it.'

I think we are a bit prudish in England. A lot of sex therapy comes too late and there's too much talking about it, instead of doing it. Perhaps if there were a place you could do it, rather than talk about it, certainly I think men would sort things out much quicker. Perhaps there should be sex classes in the run-up to a wedding. It would be interesting, wouldn't it? Hey, there's a gap in the market! Then, if the groom had had some experience that he really liked, but didn't know how to tell his bride, he could say that he'd learnt it in the class. That goes for her, too. Perfect!

Do you seek approval on your sexual performance?

ANDREA: Do you go for feedback, Carol? I'm sure you don't need it!

CAROL: No I don't, but I've given it in the past.

ANDREA: I'm sure you have, Carol!

CAROL: I've never actually said, 'You're rubbish.' But – in the past, not now, I might add – I have actually had to tell some people . . .

ALL: People?!!!

CAROL: ... that they're not doing it right. You have to! What is the point in pretending something is great when it's not? It's never going to get any better, is it? No, I think I have done a great service to womankind actually, because it means that those blokes that I've told how to do it properly are now going around doing it for women and doing it properly. So everyone wins.

ANDREA: They might even still have that little diagram you drew for them.

CAROL: I did give one of them a diagram! Honestly, he really didn't know. But that's fine. He was happy.

ANDREA: I have asked for feedback once, because I'm not that experienced in numbers, as it were. Steve is more experienced in numbers, so I asked him if maybe there was something that other people had done that maybe he would like me to do.

SHERRIE: Did you?

CAROL: What, you asked him for a checklist?

ANDREA: Not exactly, no.

COLEEN: And what did he say?

ANDREA: He said, 'No, you're all right, sweetheart.'

COLEEN: He is such a creep!

Do women underestimate
male performance anxiety?

SHERRIE: I wouldn't know. It's not something I've ever thought about and I have never spoken to a man about it. It would never have occurred to me. I suppose people get nervous. That sort of topic never comes up with my gay friends. They don't talk to me about sex.

COLEEN: I don't know either, because I've never come across it – if you'll pardon the pun! None of my friends have mentioned it either, so maybe that's just something they don't want to talk about, because their husbands wouldn't want me to know that much about it. It's never occurred to me. Also, I'm married to a man with whom I'd discuss that if it happened. This is how it would go. Him: 'I can't do it.' Me: 'Good, because I want to go to sleep! Let's hope you can't for a while . . .'

DENISE: I feel really, really sorry for men in that department. There are two things about being a man that I would hate. One is not being able to improve myself with make-up in the morning. Imagine looking in the mirror in the morning and thinking, Well, that's just me! It doesn't bear thinking about. And the other is not being able to perform. Women know that we can pretend, if need be. It's sad if you have to go through your whole life pretending, but at least we can. They can't.

So it would be awful to meet someone like me, someone who is not very tolerant of a man not performing well. Actually, that's not true – what I mean to say is that I wouldn't stay in a relationship where it happened regularly from the start. But not in a million years would I be rude. I'd pretend that

'I, I don't know what happened. I just suddenly thought of your mother'

it was fabulous, or I would say, 'Of course it doesn't matter, for goodness sake!' I like to hope that the reason it hasn't happened many times is that I put men at their ease. After all, that's the first place nerves are going to affect in a man, isn't it? Horrendous!

I could never understand how my friends could see a guy quite clearly plucking up courage to walk over to them in a nightclub; then they'd watch him walk across the whole dance floor; and then they'd say no to him! That's why I spent half my life dancing with Quasimodo in nightclubs, because I just couldn't bear to see a man do that walk of shame away from me. Yet friends of mine didn't even flinch; they would turn him down without a second thought. Now I bet those girls are really terrifying when it comes to letting a guy know she's disappointed in his performance!

LYNDA: My first husband didn't fancy me. His was a classic case of suffering from 'good girl/bad girl' syndrome. He fancied one-night stands and 'dirty' sex; the women he slept with were all very obvious types, blonde with big tits. The minute he respected or loved a woman, he couldn't get it up. It was the same for his first wife as it was for me. Apparently it's incredibly common, in varying degrees.

Lots of young men use porn and get off on porn. Then, unfortunately for them, when it comes to the real thing, they can't get it up. I think it's because they are used to being completely uninvolved. They watch sex without partaking in it and so the minute they actually have to engage and deal with all the social aspects that go with real sex, they get confused about having 'dirty' thoughts about a 'nice' girl and their willies go limp.

Girls come on to men now with all guns blazing. Men used to have to go and pay for a blow job, but now they can get a blow job any place, any time, anywhere. A blow job means absolutely nothing now; there are no longer any connotations for the women of being a dirty sexual object. So there is nowhere to go, except back to basics, back to falling in love and kissing for an hour.

Who knows what is good sex and what is bad sex? Or who is good and who is not? Warren Beatty was regarded as a god sexually, but it seemed to be more about how many people he slept with than the quality of the sex. Men seem to think that men with big willies are better in bed than men with small ones, whereas a woman might say that big ones can be uncomfortable. If people talked about this more openly, and less competitively, we would all be better off.

LISA: I have to say, I've never been with a bloke who hasn't been able to get it up. That's not me bragging, it's just been my experience. In fact, it's a bit of a nuisance sometimes, because everyone I've been out with always wants it all the time. I find it a little bit annoying, because it's not on my agenda sometimes. I've got other things I need to do! I want to slap it down or put it in a door, get rid of it – proverbially, at least. I don't know if men think, Isn't it great? I can get an erection! But I've not been out with a bloke who can't get one. For me, it's more that it's really annoying that they have them all the time.

Would you be offended if a man rolled over after sex?

LISA: As long as it's afterwards, it's fine! Well, doesn't everybody?

SHERRIE: That's the whole idea.

LISA: You could just make me feel comfortable and say yes, Sherrie! I think it is supposed to relax you, isn't it? I know I keep going on about being busy but I do think just sort of rolling over is OK at the end of the day, if you're tired. I suppose it's different if you're in a hotel on holiday and you've got time to shoot the breeze and have a chat about it afterwards.

SHERRIE: I think the thing with me is that I used to start a conversation, do it, and then carry on talking afterwards. He'd be asleep and I wouldn't be bothered, so no wonder I'm not married anymore!

ZOE: For me, I think it's rude. Don't fall asleep! I want a cuddle and a bit of a chat. He has to stay up at least fifteen minutes for the second go! Actually, on one particularly horrible occasion I realized that they don't fall asleep, because they are in the bathroom, phoning their other half!

LISA: God, that's a scary admission Zoe!

ZOE: Only joking! Although it has happened before . . .

Is seduction purely a female art, or are men also skilled seducers?

LYNDA: Men seduce women in obvious ways by plying them with champagne and buying roses and giving compliments. They are much simpler than we are, and I don't mean that in a derogatory way. Women are much more manipulative and scheming.

LISA: I think a man's idea of seduction is very different to our idea of seduction. For me, it's making me laugh; it's an emotional connection; it's probably got very little to do with lying horizontal next to anybody. It's dinner and being playful and the thoughts that are connecting with bits of your body. Seduction, for me, is not being able to have something.

Men tend to do the things that inevitably lead up to sex. It's usually something like a hand on a breast or a hand down your pants. It's cut to the chase, for them. For women, it's more about the thought and not being able to.

LYNDA: Sexually, I think is really interesting that if I make a pass at my hubby and he is really not in the mood, then that is it. Whereas if he makes a pass at me when I'm not in the mood, I can still think, 'OK. You start and I'll join in!'

I think all young men should go with an older women at some point. And perhaps there are things that young women could learn from a prostitute or a courtesan that might benefit a relationship. There was a brief time where health workers were teaching women to put condoms on in creative, erotic ways. That was an absolutely brilliant idea: using femininity and sexuality in a really positive, self-worth affirming, life saving way. It seemed much more honest and sexually interesting than the facts of life or biology lessons.

COLEEN: Lynda Bellingham! Sometimes you say the most outrageous things! With Ray, I seduced him. Normally I would be mortified at the idea of making the first move, but for the first time I thought to myself, you're a grown up: get over it! Maturity helps, as a woman, because you become more confident. I was thirty-five when I met Ray. Had I been twenty-five, there's no way I would have done it.

I went round to his flat and he'd made me dinner, which was nice. Then we sat on the couch. 'Do you want to watch a film?' he asked. 'What would you like to watch?' At that point I thought, come on, now. We know where this is leading. Let's not put a film in between us for two hours. I've told the kids I'm working; I need to get back! And if you don't want to do it, I'll just go home!

'I'd rather just see your bedroom,' I said.

He took a deep breath and said, 'OK, then!'

I knew what was going to happen, because we fancied each other massively. I was mad about him from day two. Meanwhile he was probably thinking, she's a woman: I'm going to have to do some groundwork, do the whole movie thing. But I thought, oh, I'm so past that!

LYNDA: Which movie was he planning to put on?

COLEEN: It would definitely have been some romantic girly thing. I think men make more of an effort when you first meet, don't they? I don't think he would have put *Terminator 3* on. That would be a passion killer!

DENISE: Oh God! Can you imagine? You'd be asleep. When I was younger and single, men were always able to seduce me by being gorgeous looking, period. But as I get older, I am seduced by humour. I found that the greatest seduction tool is laughter and the best way to seduce a woman is by laughing them into bed.

LYNDA: I love to make men laugh. That's very sexy. It's also a relief to them to be able to laugh. You never find sex funny when you are young. God, it is so serious! But now what turns me on is the humour. Where is the most ridiculous place you could have it? The laughter can become very sexual.

COLEEN: Have you ever actively gone out to seduce a man?

LISA: I can't do all that fluttering eyelashes and sexy nightie thing, but I'm coming around to the sexy underwear thing. I always thought that it didn't matter what you were wearing. If your body looked crap, then what did it matter if you'd spent hundreds of pounds on underwear? I would rather have seen a clean white crisp g-string on a perfectly toned tanned body than a body in a La Perla bra and panties that's going to flap all over the shop when it's being active. Paul wants to buy me underwear and he doesn't care how much it costs, but I still feel it's a bit of a waste of money.

DENISE: Perhaps you should give it a try! Years ago, I remember setting my cap at people and going all out to get them. But perhaps some women make it more obvious than others. Like you, Lisa, I'm not all fluttering behind a fan. If the eye contact didn't work, then I'd just go over and ask them.

LYNDA: That direct approach rarely fails! What I find interesting is that there is a kind of intellectual man who is very easy to seduce because you basically go straight for the blow job, which will blow their minds. In my experience, if you look curvaceous, you are not taken seriously by an intellectual man. But actually they are the easiest to seduce, because they haven't owned up to their animal instincts. If you open them up in that way, they will be yours for life.

I think Marilyn Monroe tried to get to Arthur Miller cerebrally, but because her image was of an air-headed sex symbol, she never got credit for it. The attraction for him was her complete sexuality. But she didn't really believe in her sexuality and at the same time was insecure that she wasn't an intellectual. Had she enjoyed and accepted her universal sexuality, there might not have been a problem.

In the past, if you wanted to pull some of the intellectual men in the theatre that I've come across, you had to be a body, but dress down and pretend you weren't, while in bed you'd somehow have learnt to give a man a blow job. It's the 'Miss Jones, you are a beautiful woman!' syndrome. It's still very prevalent, I think.

COLEEN: Have you ever thought about writing a sex guide, Lynda? Because if you haven't, you should!

Are fantasies a good sex tool?

LYNDA: I don't think much of all that business about having fantasies. If you're thinking about someone else while he is on top of you, that's not good sex. It has to be eye to eye between you. That's good sex. Otherwise you lose that contact and connection. Anyway, I don't think I could ever have somebody inside me while I was thinking about somebody else. I've never done it. I can happily be chatted up by a man or contemplate going to bed with a man – because I'm either getting over someone or trying to make somebody jealous – but I couldn't actually go on to have sex in those circumstances.

DENISE: Do you think you would know if a man was thinking of someone else?

LYNDA: I don't know. I'd like to think I'd know. If I knew his history, I might have that in my mind and suffer the insecurity of worrying that he was thinking of her. We do that to each other a lot, don't we? We impose these other things on our boyfriends, lovers and husbands either to punish or torment ourselves, rather than just letting it be.

Then again, I know people who have been in relationships for years and then found out that their other half has been unfaithful, and the biggest, hardest thing for them is that it ruins that whole relationship for them. They assume that their other halves were lying to them the whole time and that all those years were for nothing. It must be terrible. It's not much comfort, but I don't think it's true in that kind of situation that your partner lied all the time. They did love you, but could also go off and do other things.

LISA: Like you, Lynda, I'm not very good with fantasies. I feel like it's a bit of a betrayal. I don't get that thing of having sex with someone and imagining you're having it with someone else! To me, that is almost tantamount to being unfaithful.

I love you too . . . Brad

Does sex mean something different to men and women?

COLEEN: I think sex is so different for men and women. Men can separate it from any form of emotional bonding; it's purely sex. That's why, especially when they're drunk and with a group of lads, men can sleep with anything. Whether it's because their bits are on the outside and it's not quite as personal for them as it is for us, I don't know.

I know it's different for Denise and Carol. When I read their autobiographies, my mouth dropped open. Oh my God! I couldn't get over it. It doesn't mean I don't love them, though.

Denise and I are very alike in that we agree that men and women are different. I'm not threatened when Ray says, 'Blooming heck, she's nice!' I don't think, oh, he doesn't love me; he doesn't fancy me. I point girls out in the street and say, 'Look at her. Great bum,' or, 'Great legs.'

But Denise said something in her book about being a gay man in a woman's body. She can look at sex in a detached way, whereas I would have to really fancy someone, really like them and think that there's potential for a relationship before I slept with them. I couldn't just pick someone up in a bar.

I tried it twice in my life, when I was very young. I thought, I can be like a big, strong independent woman. We were tipsy, we were flirting and we knew we were going to have sex; it was never going to be any more than that. I thought I could handle it, but I hated it. I didn't enjoy it and I didn't feel good about myself.

LYNDA: Why did you do it the second time, then? Just to make sure?

COLEEN: The first time was just after my first long term relationship ended. I was nearly nineteen and heartbroken. I was on tour and I thought, so what? I can still pull! And I suppose I kind of wanted it to get back to my ex. It was immature of me. The guy I pulled was lovely but the experience was horrible.

The second time was in Australia. The guy was absolutely beautiful, just stunning. All my sisters noticed him. 'Isn't he gorgeous?' they said. But he was looking at me! It was the night before we went back to England, so it was a case of now or never. So I did! He was a marine, as well. I just wish I'd seen him in uniform, because he was stunning out of uniform! I don't actually regret that one, but it still made me realise that one-night stands weren't for me. He wrote to me several times after that, actually. I never replied to him. What's the point if he's in Australia? I was never going to see him again.

SHERRIE: Yes, but you might have actually seen him in uniform! You cannot beat a naval officer or an RAF officer's uniform. That totally does it for me.

How much does it bother us if our men look at other women?

ZOE: You know what? It doesn't really bother me. I was brought up with my mum watching things like James Bond films and saying, 'Oh God, he's gorgeous!' It seemed normal to me. Then I had a relationship with somebody who took huge offence to me commenting on anybody at all, even if they were on TV. So I became confused about whether it was right or wrong, to be honest. But men can't help it, can they? We've all had a conversation with a man whose eyes are following another woman across the room. They can't help it, because their brains are lower than ours!

SHERRIE: Yes, and sometimes they don't talk to your eyes, they just look down and talk to your boobs, don't they? I had an ex who did it all the time. I don't actually know what it's like to have a man who you can really trust.

DENISE: Would you be threatened if you saw your fella looking at a lads' mag?

LISA: I'd rather he took himself off somewhere and did it on his own, whatever he was doing. I think I'd be more offended by the fact he didn't try to hide it. But I don't mind Page 3 and stuff. Paul would probably look at it and say, 'She's got a nice figure.' And I'd probably say, 'Yes, she's got a very nice figure.'

DENISE: What if he watched porn?

LISA: I wouldn't like it. I'm sure it doesn't go on in my house. I was going to say that I'm sure it does go on, but I think he would be offended if he read that! I don't think of it as a betrayal or like someone being unfaithful, but I don't like it.

SHERRIE: It insults you a little bit, because it makes you feel second best. I couldn't cope with it.

LISA: It's not so much that. I think what is offensive about it is that I like to think my partner is more intelligent than that.

SHERRIE: It's not to do with intelligence though, is it?

LISA: Well, I'm quite lucky he's not a boob man anyway, because I wouldn't even be in the race! Strangely, he is only ever really interested in that area when he is ill. I think it's a mother thing. He says, 'If only!' I say, 'Well, I can push them together and make one good one!'

ZOE: It's a balance. Looking at somebody else is fine as long as they are respectful to you and not taking it any further. Then it's fine. As long as you know they love you and they are with you and just you.

DENISE: I just say to Tim, 'Oh you are pathetic!' Because he tries to do this rubbish cover-up. We'll be driving along and he'll cough guiltily. 'Why do you have to sound like you suddenly have TB, just because you have seen some girl's bum out the window?' Do you know what I mean?

SHERRIE: To be truthful, we all do it. I mean, we all look at beautiful guys.

DENISE: I do it all the time!

LISA: Interestingly, Paul doesn't like it if there is a naked torso on the telly and I'm having a bit of a linger. It's funny that they don't like it either!

DENISE: Lisa, you say you'd be cross if he didn't hide what he was doing. But if they don't mention things and they haven't talked about them, then you think, hang on a minute. Why did you not mention this? Beware the type of guy who looks at Page 3 and throws it aside in disgust. He's the kind who would pretend not to notice when a naked woman walks through the room. Those sorts of men are the ones to watch, believe me! Not the ones who are doing it openly.

Can a man impress you with his physical prowess?

COLEEN: I remember when I was a teenager hearing boys say things like, 'I'm a bit tired, because I only managed 200 press ups this morning.' Then his mate would say, 'Really? I did 300.' They always have to be bigger and better, with their chests puffed out. I can't bear it! I wish someone could get it through to them. Even with my sons sometimes, or their friends, I want to shout, 'Stop it! Just stop it! You are not impressing the girls. They think you are an idiot.'

ANDREA: It's primal, isn't it?

COLEEN: I can't bear it; I find it such a turn off.

DENISE: Obviously Tim lured me in with his physical prowess, as I'm sure you will all understand. So when I go to the gym for my once-a-year trip, I can be quite moved, shall I say, by someone showing their physical prowess off in that way. Not

*Darren had been convinced that his JLS dance routine
would finally win Emma from Accounts over . . .*

that I would necessarily want to be married to that person, but for half an hour, it would be champion!

ANDREA: Too much pressure.

COLEEN: Half an hour?

DENISE: You could get it done in half an hour, in the gym.

COLEEN: Five minutes!

DENISE: Tim does show off a bit. He was in the parachute regiment, right? In about 1926. So nobody can ever say anything about anything to do with fitness or aeroplanes, without him saying, 'Well, of course, I've done 13 jumps from higher than this!' He's always saying it. 'No one is interested,' I tell him.

He also thinks that the body has a memory for fitness, which apparently it really does. He takes that to extremes though. 'You're 58,' I say, 'and you're talking about when you were 19. Your body doesn't have such a good a memory that it means you don't have to go to the gym anymore!'

ANDREA: But showing off does start very young. My son Findley, bless him, is only eight and he loves skateboarding. But if we happen to be out and the little girl he likes in his class turns up, all of a sudden he goes from being pretty normal to skating into a wall or falling on the floor or hitting himself and shouting, 'Ha ha ha!' Although I suppose it doesn't really change as they get older . . .

COLEEN: They don't stop showing off.

LYNDA: It's like cars, isn't it? Why do Ferraris always have old men in them? Showing off!

My sons were going to the match the other day. They are Arsenal supporters, but that's not to be held against them. They were walking along the pavement and there were some lads passing in a car, revving madly and mocking them for being Arsenal supporters. Well, these lads were so busy revving up and taking the mick, 'Nah nah, na-na nah!' that the driver drove straight into the back of the car in front.

So my sons had that magical moment of being able to yell, 'Nah nah, na-na nah!' back at them.

ANDREA: You see! They don't get older, they just get taller.

Does a man's sex drive diminish in a long-term relationship?

LYNDA: Everything comes and goes, but I don't see why your sex drive should diminish in a long-term relationship. It's just that sometimes it's stronger than at other times.

Many couples split up when the children leave home. In a perfect world, you'd get married, have your children and bring them up together and then as your marriage starts to wane, head off for a year, go mad and have lots of sex with other people. Then you come back to the person you love and cherish and you are up for it again, for the last twenty years. That could be the answer.

When I met and married Michael, I was at that stage when

the children have grown up and left home, and you are left facing retirement.

When a man retires, he can lose his purpose in life; he invades his wife's space. Everybody needs to be taken in hand at this moment; the situation needs to be reviewed, because people find they have nothing in common.

To be honest, it's down to luck that you move along parallel paths and learn similar life experiences, especially if you are a woman and you have been bringing up children. If you find a yawning gap between you, then you should perhaps have a 'gap' year, or even better go travelling together. It changes everything just to look different, the way you do when you're on holiday. Dress up in a toga! Just view the other person completely differently. This is another thing worth talking about. The more we can bring the problem out in the open and talk about it in society, the fewer people will feel isolated and think it's only them suffering.

After a long period of celibacy, can it ever be too late to get back into having sex?

DENISE: Women who've had no sex for a long time are probably very self-conscious about their body and things going southward. But it's nothing that a couple of bottles of Blossom Hill wouldn't help! To me it's like riding a bike. If it was something you enjoyed, I don't think it would take very long to get back in the saddle.

Quite a few of my friends have met people through the

internet and I think that's a really safe, sensible way to do it if you're an older women. One of my best friends is now living with someone that she met through the internet. I don't think it's remotely sad, whereas I think there is nothing sadder than older people hanging around in nightclubs hoping to meet someone, or sitting at home feeling lonely.

What I couldn't be bothered with is having to go through all that baggage again. I'd want to know if someone has children, and if they smoke and all of those things, without all the fannying around. With the internet, you can find out all those things about the person before you decide to meet them. I think it would be quite fun, looking to see who has sent you a message. You probably have to email or 'poke' a few frogs, but it's better than kissing them!

The other night, a friend of mine had a call from her ninety-year-old granny in New Zealand to say that she had two men chasing her in her retirement home. When my friend asked her why she had finished with the last guy, she said, 'Because it was all grope, grope, grope, all the time!' She still has an active sex life at ninety, which is amazing, but this guy was a groper and she didn't like it. Made me laugh!

CAROL: I didn't mind living without sex. I think you just switch off. I actually found that my life was much less complicated without it, because it tends to cloud your thoughts and your judgement. You become, not obsessed . . . but distracted. Now I am sexually active again, I can't believe I went seven years without it. But at the time you don't think about it. What you don't have, you don't miss. You get used to not doing it.

I also think that if a woman wants to have sex, it's very easy to get someone to do it with her. So in a way, I was choosing not to. I could have got off with someone if I'd wanted to, but I just didn't want to. I was quite happy not to do it.

My mum died in 2003 and everything switched off. When we came back to *Loose Women* in the summer of 2004, I couldn't even talk about sex. It was totally off my radar. I wasn't interested at all. Something inside you dies when you lose someone you love, for a while, at least. My mum was the most important person in my world. She had such a massive influence on my life. She was the first person I really knew and loved who died. I was probably quite lucky to get to 43 without knowing anybody who had died. Luckily, time does heal. You learn to live with it, but it took me about three years to wake up again. One of my friends was the same. Her mum died about the same time as my mum, and she didn't have any relationships for three years. I don't think it's conscious. You don't even think about it. It just happens.

LYNDA: Quite a number of women have come up to me after seeing me in *Calendar Girls* on stage and said something like, 'I'm sixty-five and I've just been waiting to die, really. But now I've seen you taking your clothes off in the play, I'm thinking that perhaps there is a life out there for me.'

'Of course there is a life out there for you!' I say. 'Not all men want to marry young girls. There are men like my husband who would rather have an older woman.'

As much as we don't look like we did when we were twenty, it's also possible not to be grey-haired at sixty, or stuck in an unflattering long skirt. Recently I was wearing a favourite above-the-knee red dress and a woman said to me, 'After seeing you, I may just get my legs out again.' 'Yes, get them out!' I said.

DENISE: Good advice!

LYNDA: It can be so hard to get your confidence back. A friend of mine has just been through a terrible divorce. Her ex-husband destroyed her by going off with a younger model. He was her life and it has affected her on every level; she is in her late-fifties and she has lost her partner and her home. Everything has fallen apart and she has had to start again.

She had grey hair all their married life because he said that he liked it grey. Meanwhile, we all thought, 'I wish she'd dye her hair.' She dyed it instantly after he left and she looked ten years younger. She also lost lots of weight and bought some really nice clothes. She went on the dating websites and initially met up with slightly suspect young men; it turned out that a couple of them were having every single woman in her area!

Still, she has found somebody now. I admire her so much for getting out there. She is really up for sex, because she had a good sex life in her marriage and she misses it. The only problem is that the man she is with now is in his late-sixties and she thinks he is old. It's different when you have grown old with your partner, because you tend to see each other as you were when you first met.

SHERRIE: Another problem is that when you're a strong personality, it's hard to let a man in because you take up all of your space. There's none going spare. You miss love, affection and a cuddle, of course you do; I miss that desperately. But you can learn to live without it. You have to. That is why I have always had animals, because they give you unconditional love. However, recently I made the decision not to have any more animals. I am devoted to animals, but I no longer want commitments, apart from my child and my grandchild. Not even a budgie!

LYNDA: And there's a big difference between a budgie and a man! Returning to the subject of sex, I have a friend who hasn't had a relationship for about twenty years and she's said to me that she thinks she has probably sealed up. For all this time, she just hasn't met anybody who does it for her, which is extraordinary, because she is incredibly attractive, even now she's older. Actually, she could have done it a couple of times, but she didn't follow it through. If she had, she would have kept things going.

I've always gone out there and embraced it all. A lot of that was probably to do with drink, but the point is not to miss the moment! It probably helps to have the odd drunken foray every now and then. Times have changed; you no longer have to feel like a slapper or a hussy. Who cares? It's not like in your youth when people couldn't wait to expose you, so if you reach a certain age and you want to have a drunken fumble, bloody hell go ahead and have it! Nobody needs to know about it. If you don't see the man again, it doesn't matter. When you get older, you cross a line and suddenly life has become short. So you better get on with it.

I've talked to my gynaecologist about whether she could really have 'sealed up'. He said that sex can be painful for a woman who hasn't had it for a long time. So, how can we keep things going when we're single? How can you keep yourself up for it and make sure your body stays in tune? Vibrators might be an answer for some women; your sexuality is not

Audrey's heart sank as her hand luggage set off the security system.
'My oh my, it . . . it must be my electric toothbrush . . .' she stuttered

dependent on men and you don't have to have a rampant sex life to be sexual. On the other hand, without an ongoing sex life, it's difficult to sit there and persuade yourself that you're marvellously attractive. The affirmation that men give is often crucial to feeling sexy.

SHERRIE: Yes, a budgie can't really help in that area!

Do men even notice cellulite on women?

LYNDA: I find that women are much more critical than men about other women. When we try to say what a man fancies, we are doing it through a woman's eye. We think that men only fancy girls with perfect tits, but it's utterly untrue. I don't think men even knew what cellulite was until magazines started highlighting it. It's women writing those articles, not men. How many men have you heard say that they like to have something to get hold of? They don't want a skinny model. If they did, the human race would not have survived!

I feel comfortable with men because I don't feel they are looking at me in the way that women sometimes do. They're not thinking, 'God, you're fat. You're not very attractive.'

DENISE: Our hang-ups are desperately sad and I think men, quite rightly, switch off when we start banging on. If I were a man, I would tire of us. We're so boring! I include myself in that statement; in fact, I'm at the top of the list. 'Does my bum look big?' I say. 'Do you like the blue or the red? The blue? That means you hate the red!' Thank God they don't do it too! It would drive me mad if I was with a man who talked about his looks all the time.

Our obsession with cellulite and being stick thin is ridiculous. We know for a fact that our men don't fancy us thin. The only men who want us to be thin are usually gay and/or in the fashion industry. Apart from Gok Wan of course, who is gay *and* in the fashion industry. Fashion people love stick thin women because clothes looks so great on them, but red-blooded men don't want women with that type of figure, so why do we aspire to it? Why do we worry so much? Why do we torture ourselves about our cellulite, if the men we're with don't mind? If, like me, you're not often going to get your wobbly legs out on the beach anymore, does it really matter that much, if you can buy clothes to cover it up?

I've tried to analyse it, but the phases in my life when I've been aware of male attention, as opposed to those phases when I've felt invisible, don't seem to depend on whether I am a stone heavier or lighter. So why do I get so upset about being a stone heavier than I want to be, when it is clearly not affecting my attractiveness to men? Yes, I might be 'doing it for me' when I try to lose weight, but ultimately we all want to go out and be found attractive by men. Anybody who says they don't is usually fibbing.

At the same time, I recognise that I'm the one who has had eye surgery; I'm the one who has just seen a DVD of a pilot programme I've made and wants to jump in the River Tyne; and I'm the one now researching the best plastic surgeons in the UK! It's a complete contradiction.

COLEEN: We worry about it because other women are always pointing it out. I think we're our own worst enemies when it comes to body issues. We all do it and the media does it even more. Celebrity women are always being papped without their make-up or with unwashed hair, but men rarely are. Every event covered by the papers and magazines has a section called, 'Who's the best dressed?' Two pages of the good dresses; two pages of the bad dresses; and nothing about the men who turned up looking dreadful.

We're the ones that read it. We love saying, 'Oh my God, have you seen Pamela Anderson's cellulite? I'm so happy!' It makes us think there's hope for us! The fact that I put paparazzi pictures of women Ray likes on my fridge door, so that he sees them every time he opens the fridge, says it all. 'You see?' I say. 'She looks crap without make-up and there are dimples in her bum!'

He laughs when he sees me in magazine shoots, looking beautiful. 'Christ, that took some doing!' he'll tease. 'Good bit of airbrushing there, Col!' 'Eh, don't knock it,' I say. 'It's the best invention ever. Never mind banning it. More, please!'

SHERRIE: It's not just women. Some men are very critical of the way women look. My ex-husband was. He liked very tall and thin women; he didn't like women with curves. He would always notice if a woman had a vein on her leg or cellulite. He was just as critical of himself, I have to say. He was very conscious of his looks and his body. Aesthetically, something had to be beautiful in his eyes. If it wasn't, then it was ugly. There was no half way, so you didn't stand a chance, especially as you got older.

Some men are very accepting and say, 'Well, that is part of you.' Whether they're lying or not, I don't know, but it sounds good!

LISA: If you're in your forties and you're with a man who is in his forties, the chances are he's ageing as well, so the chances are that all your bits are falling apart at the same time. So that's quite nice! In your twenties, it eats away at you. If only you could impart what you know now to a 20-year-old and say, 'Actually, it really isn't that important.' But no one of 20 is going to listen!

The sexiest women are those that, regardless of body shape, are just as at home in their own skin. The great thing about being a Loose Woman is that you're open about your faults and you share them. It's very liberating to be able to celebrate the things that for years you thought were holding you back! In fact, the only thing holding you back is the fact that you think it's holding you back.

Are men as hung up about their looks as women are?

COLEEN: Yes, I think men are vain. It's weird though, because they hate going grey, but they don't want to dye their hair because their mates will take the mick out of them. I don't understand it: my brothers and brothers-in-law are all that way. I want to say to them, 'So you would rather look ten years older than have your mate say, "Ha, you've dyed your hair!"' I would rather say, 'Yes, I've dyed my hair, so that I don't look like you!' Why wouldn't you cover traces of grey? Just because your mates will accuse you of being vain? Men are strange like that, and yet they worry about it.

I'm never going to be grey, not even when I'm ninety-five,

because I think it ages you. Of course, it suits certain people. Philip Schofield looks great. He's got that lovely silver-grey hair. I still think he would look younger if he dyed his hair, but I've got used to him now.

DENISE: Men also worry; I just don't think that they talk about it as much. A man in the pub with a beer belly and love handles won't be saying, 'Oh my God, I can't believe I'm having another pint! Will you look at the love handles on me?' He won't be drawing attention to himself in that way. He will be thinking it, though; he just won't be sharing it.

Men should be bothered about what they look like, but I have some male friends who can't walk past a mirror without looking at it. I was married to someone who couldn't pick up his knife and fork without looking at his reflection in them. There is a happy medium somewhere between Tim and cutlery mirror guy. I like men to take an active interest, but not take it too far!

LISA: I think men cotton on to the fact that women are interested in a certain look, initially. If you're going on first impressions, then looks really do count.

Chapter 4

Men: the inside story

'CAN'T YOU TRY BEING A BIT MORE ROMANTIC?'

Still mystified by the inner workings of the male brain? Join the club! Although we're convinced that we're far more complex than men are, they're still not very easy to figure out, are they? There are all these stereotypes about them – they think about sex all the time; they're less intuitive than we are; they can't talk about their feelings or multitask – but are any of them true? And can you really get what you want from him by cooking up his favourite meal?

It would take a legion of psychologists and behavioural therapists to figure out what men are all about, but we reckon we've got them sussed, at least in some areas. There's no denying the differences between us, of course. They don't gossip in the same way that we do and they're often rubbish at being romantic. They have a different way of getting over relationship break-ups and they cry at different things, if they cry at all. And, boy, can they be boring when they're drunk! (Whereas we're tipsily witty and charming, ahem.)

How important is it to understand men fully, though? Does it matter if we look at each other blankly from time to time, unable to fathom what the blooming heck the other one is going on about? It takes years to get to know them and even then they can still surprise us, thank goodness. Otherwise life just might become a teensy weensy bit boring, especially after a whole summer of footie and blaring vuvuzelas, followed by a winter of total premier league obsession. Grrr!

Is the way to a man's heart through his stomach?

DENISE: Well, certainly not in my case. I would never have had the boyfriends or the partners that I've had if feeding them had anything to do with it. I mean, honest to God, I must have cooked ten meals in my life for people I've been going out with. So I must have been offering plus points in different areas!

Luckily, I've never met anyone who has been disappointed that I can't cook. Instead I go for people who can cook. My sister and I both made it a priority that we would marry people who cooked, more for the sake of feeding our children than feeding ourselves, because I'd be happy to just go out all the time or get takeaways.

SHERRIE: When I was married, if I wanted to do something and I knew that my husband would question it, I would buy him a large Aberdeen Angus steak. Then I would grill it with English mustard and brown sugar, so that all the mustard and sugar would melt into the meat.

He would do anything if I gave him steak done that way.

'Right, I've booked a holiday,' I'd say. 'OK, fine by me,' he'd say.

So it wasn't sex that won the day, it was Aberdeen Angus Steak with mustard and sugar. He never smelt a rat, either. He just thought, I'm getting an Aberdeen Angus steak, so it's all right with me. It never occurred to him I could have been having an affair with the butcher!!

COLEEN: Sounds delicious! I would probably do anything for you, Sherrie, if you made that for me. You wouldn't even have to bother with the honey glaze.

ANDREA: Does your cooking have the same effect on Ray, Col?

COLEEN: You're joking! Ray definitely wouldn't do something for me once he'd tasted my cooking.

LISA: I can't cook, either! I'm rubbish. I know good food from bad, though – and that's half my problem, because I know when something tastes terrible! I couldn't serve up what I cook, because I wouldn't want to eat it, so I couldn't expect anyone else to! Luckily, Paul always says, 'I didn't marry you for your cooking.' But then again, he's never actually married me, so I don't know what that means!

DENISE: I love food but I don't see it in an aphrodisiac sort of way. Tim and I are not foodie people and we certainly don't ever recreate the *Nine and a Half Weeks* Kim Basinger/ Mickey Rourke moment with food. But he cooks me wonderful comfort food: either his cheese and egg pasta bake or his special pie will always do the trick.

Do men think about sex all the time?

LISA: Yes, I think they probably do . . .

LYNDA: Of course men think about sex all of the time. It is hysterical! Without a doubt they do, every however many seconds it is. Sometimes you can catch them and they know you know. Either they are embarrassed or they laugh.

I remember my father saying to me, 'Men are animals.' 'You are not an animal, Daddy!' I said. It was fantastic that he could recognise and say such a thing. Of course, women are animals too, but they are much less aggressive and much more manipulative. Even a lioness is submissive in a mating situation. She can be aggressive if she needs to defend her children, but she is not sexually aggressive. The most powerful women don't get power by grabbing it; they do it completely differently to men, by using their sexuality.

Can men ever talk about their emotions?

SHERRIE: I'm sure that there are lots of men out there who do talk about their feelings, but I've never met them. The men I've known didn't want to talk about emotions. They didn't want to talk at all. Everything you said was nagging. You were supposed to be quiet and agree with them. Anything that came close to the point of saying, 'Let's discuss this,' triggered shut-down time. Men don't like to talk and discuss. 'Just leave it,' they say. Generally, they're not like us.

We have to talk through everything in our lives. That's why *Loose Women* is successful. Men appear not to have to, or they must do it in their heads, because I don't think they do it down the pub. I don't know when they get all this stuff out. They must shut it down. I assume that is what is wrong emotionally with a lot of men. At least we get it out.

DENISE: I do think men are crap about talking about their feelings. People have said to us over the years, 'Why don't you have *Loose Men?*' Believe you me, it has been mooted and it's been taken on board several times. But when we've done pilots, men just don't want to talk about themselves. They turn everything into a joke.

On *Loose Women,* the humour often derives from stories about ourselves. We are not scared to open up about ourselves, whereas the men didn't like it when we tried to delve. They just wanted to disarm everyone with jokes, but *Loose Women* is not just about telling jokes, it's about talking about yourself. Men are not as comfortable doing that, especially not English men. I haven't had much experience of American men, but I suspect that American men are slightly more open – maybe not with their friends, but they nearly all have a therapist, so they are talking to somebody about it.

Men are just not interested enough in the minutiae of life. There's so much said about men bragging about their sex lives, but I think women talk much more about sex than men do. Tim would be horrified with some of the things that I've talked about! I honestly don't think he has a friend with whom he would discuss that kind of thing.

He has friends he can talk to when we have had problems and thank goodness for that. But we talk about men even when we're just popping out to see *Sex and the City*. They never would.

A couple of years ago, Tim did an episode of *George Gently*, starring Martin Shaw. He was on it for about a fortnight and had a really nice guest lead in it. He would call me on a nightly basis, talking about how he was getting on really well with Martin Shaw; they were having a fantastic time together. When he came back, I said, 'So what's his wife like and where do his family live?' He had no idea! After being with him on a daily basis for a fortnight, he couldn't name Martin Shaw's children, but he knew every car that he had owned since about 1922, including the types of tyres and engines each car had. That just summed men up to me.

LYNDA: In Australia they have started a thing called 'Sheds'. They are clubs for men, mostly of retirement age, and they've been set up because there are a lot of suicides at that stage in life, because men can't talk about their feelings. In these clubs, men can talk to each other while they're learning new skills like bricklaying and woodwork. They have been a huge success; I heard a radio programme about them and one man was saying how he had cried and talked about all sorts of things he had never spoken of before.

DENISE: What is it with men and sheds?

LISA: I don't know! My partner Paul doesn't need to go into a shed in order to talk about his feelings, but that's because he came from a family of talkers. His mother and father were open about everything with him and his sister. There was no shame in showing how you felt, whatever it may be. So that's where he got it from.

My family was the opposite. No one in my family was very open. My grandmother and grandfather, who were in fact my mother and father figures, didn't show each other any affection at all. They weren't demonstrative. It was only when my grandfather was drunk that he showed my nan any affection. Then she'd laugh and say, 'Get off, silly b******!'

My granddad didn't talk about his feelings and I thought a man had to be like he was. So sometimes I'm a little emotionally shut down to the idea of Paul wanting to open up about stuff. I say to him, 'Why don't you just get on with it?'

'Well, I want to talk to you and see how you feel about it,' he'll say. 'I think we should make the decision together.'

Perhaps as a hangover from my childhood, I think, well, you're the man: you make that decision!

Paul will say, 'I don't want to make it on my own.'

And I'll say, 'Be a man about it!'

The thing is though, I was attracted to him from the start, knowing that he was a very open, honest, sensitive man. What I adore about Paul is that he's a complete creative. He loves poetry. I love it when he's explaining to Beau why a certain poem works. At school, he wasn't interested in football and he still isn't, thank God!

I think I recognised early on that someone in our relationship had to be emotionally open and I knew I was always quite self-contained in that way. I don't know whether it's a trust thing or what, but I played my cards close to my chest and I think that may have come from my grandfather. That generation said, 'Don't tell everybody your business. Just get on with it. Put up and shut up.' That applied to women, particularly – every day of the week. I saw it as a form of strength, but as I grew older, I realised that actually it's a form of weakness.

I didn't understand why you need to share these things. I didn't realise that you're missing out on the beauty and the wonderful connection you make when you share with somebody. And if you get really adept at hiding something for long enough, it becomes something totally different.

DENISE: How do you mean?

LISA: If you keep putting a little problem away, it can manifest itself in very strange ways. Then it can grow into a massive issue that you have to break down before you get to the root of it. That can take years and some people never get to the core of a problem before they die.

DENISE: When did you first realise that?

LISA: It was probably something to do with working with actors and free spirits who believe in communicating honestly and being non-judgemental. I've learned that dishonesty is the bad thing; whatever the issue is, it's fine as long as you're honest and true about it. That saved me, in a way.

Are men more competitive?

DENISE: Tim is competitive. He is not really a competitive dad, but he's a competitive husband. He honestly thinks that he can play the same roles as me! Now his dream is coming true and he is going off to become a regular in *Benidorm*, playing Leslie, a transvestite, to prove to me he can play women as well as I can.

COLEEN: Men are definitely more competitive than women. My two boys and Ray are so competitive, but I'm not at all. They all have to be the best and win anything, even on the Wii at home, the competition to get the high score is unbelievable! That's definitely more of a male trait and it shows from a very early age.

LISA: Winning contracts and winning things generally is more of a male thing. Men can be very competitive when it comes to proving their prowess on a sports field and in business. Paul is a very shrewd businessman. He's a complete dichotomy, because he's got that sensitive side and can be quite flowery, but in a business deal, all of that goes. I don't know if that's because it's all about getting the best deal to earn the money and provide for the family.

I can be competitive too, as I was reminded one day in June, when Paul and I went to pick Beau up from her rounders after-school club. It was lovely weather and we sat on the grass, in front of a running track, enjoying the summery late afternoon. After a while, we walked up to collect Beau, but she hadn't finished, so Paul said, 'I'll race you!'

'I don't want to race,' I said. But then, within about

half a breath, I'd kicked my shoes off and shouted, 'Go!' before he was ready. Actually, I'm quite a fast runner; I'm like a little whippet. So I pelted it down the running track and beat him hands down, yelling triumphantly in front of the entire rounders after-school club. Beau was really embarrassed!

Then something odd happened to me at Beau's sports day this year. Most of the mums don't go in the mums' race because they say it's a bit of a bun fight. There are even some mums who take it quite seriously and put their spikes on! Oh, those competitive mothers, what are they like? I thought. It's just a bit of fun! Well, Beau said, 'You're going in the mums' race.'

'OK,' I said. I was really nervous and psyched up, because I felt like I had to win, for Beau, because she was new at the school. Also, people kept saying, 'Are you going in the mums' race? You're really brave, aren't you?' I was so charged up!

When I got to the starting line, the headmistress came over and gave us each a balloon to put between our legs, to make it more fun. I thought, Where's the fun in that? Now we're ridiculous and we can't really have a race. In fact, what was more ridiculous was that I wanted to win the race for my daughter.

So we all started with the balloons between our legs, hobbling along for a bit. Then some people's balloons popped and they started to run. I saw one mum whip the balloon out from between her legs and start running with the balloon in her hand. I thought, right, game on! and took my balloon out. I was like Forrest Gump: 'Run, Forrest, run!' I was so nervous and charged up but I won it!

I felt rubbish afterwards. Lisa, what on earth happened

to you? I thought. Haven't you grown out of that horrible, competitive, must-win-and-be-first mentality? Aren't you a much more sedate, serene person these days? Well, no! Obviously not.

COLEEN: Women are also competitive with their looks. They want to be the best looking in the room and whatever they say, that's for the benefit of men. It's not about being better looking than your friends. If my friend is better looking than me, then what's the point in me spending hours on my hair and make-up?

My sister Maureen has always been the beautiful one out of all of us, so whatever we wear when we go out, men will always say, 'I love your sister with the dark hair.' You've spent four hours getting ready and you want to punch her, so I just tell the guys that her feet smell! 'She's got really bad feet; she's got a problem,' I say.

LISA: That's hilarious! I'm not competitive when it comes to looks at all. I'm an actor. I've appeared on screen next to twenty-somethings with flawless skin and it's been blatantly obvious who the older person is, even if I'm shrouded in frosting or there's a horse blanket over the lens! I know the help I'm getting. I'm not deluded enough to think, aren't I lovely looking? I know I've had every bit of technical help there is.

I love it when I see a beautiful young actress who's talented; it excites me. When Georgia Moffat came into *The Bill* and played my daughter, it was only her second acting role. I remember being so excited that I could see the most phenomenal acting career in front of her. She was beautiful, talented, smart, genuine, compassionate and intellectual. She had everything and it made me feel so proud. She's now like a daughter to me. She's family.

Perhaps when you're younger, you do compete, because you've got it all going on. You're expected to be beautiful; it's something you have to bring to the table. But you also learn quite quickly that you can't have anyone else's career. You'd end up insane if you sat there thinking, it's not fair! She's really beautiful and she's really successful and I'm not. As Paul says, 'There's always someone with a bigger boat.' There's always someone prettier.

Can men multitask?

COLEEN: The stereotypes of men being less intuitive and a bit crap at talking about their feelings are often right. They are not multitaskers, either. At least, Ray isn't. If I ask him to do something, he'll put in 100 per cent and he'll do it until it's finished. But if I ask him to do two things, then his whole brain jumbles. He cannot multitask, whereas I do it every single day of my life. Sometimes I go home and say, 'God, I'm knackered!' Then he'll usually say, 'You want to try being me!'

'Why, what have you done?'

'Well, I've put a wash on today and picked Ciara up from school . . .'

'Yeah, and?'

On the days I go to London to work, I get up two hours early, so that before I leave I can make sure Ciara's school uniform is washed, dried and ironed; make sure everyone else's washing is done; check there's food in the cupboard and

'*Cor, look at the bumpers on that*'

fridge; see that I've packed everything I need; make breakfast; empty the dishwasher and put another load in . . .

What I love about Ray though is that if there's something that he's got to do, he'll do it until it's finished. He's brilliant with Ciara, because he's really arty: he can paint and draw and make things out of nothing. When you've got a kid that age, that comes in handy. Recently, she had to go to school dressed as an insect and he spent six hours making her a ladybird outfit while I was away. It was fabulous. That's where we differ, because I'd just have the phone book out and be looking for a fancy dress shop!

He had to make a hat for her once and he worked so hard on it that when she went to bed, I was saying, 'It's fab; just leave it!' but he wouldn't stop until he was completely happy with it.

Are men less intuitive than women?

LISA: Paul's business instincts are very intuitive: he's good at interpreting language and body language in a complete stranger; he knows whether to trust someone; he can tell exactly what someone's intentions are.

Men are very good when they're dealing with each other, but when they're dealing with women, I think we muddy the waters so much that no one can make head or tail of it by the time we've finished! If you ask a man a question, he tends to answer that question. But a lot of the time, the question we're asking isn't actually the question we want to ask. So we're not ever going to get the answer we really want.

Men are quite black and white about it: this is the question. Now give me the answer. Women are like: here's the question, but it's not really what I mean! So they're floundering around, bless them, in the dark! Because until we know how to ask a straight question, they can't give us a straight answer.

COLEEN: You see, a woman would know what another woman was really asking. So what you're saying, Lisa, is that men are not intuitive!

LISA: With other men, they are, but not with women, no. Isn't it the same the other way around too?

Should men be knights in shining armour?

LYNDA: My dad was my absolute knight in shining armour.

LISA: That may be a good thing in a father, but I don't want a knight in shining armour as a partner! I don't want somebody to sweep me up in a flash car or onto a big stallion, declaring 'It's all right, I'm here!' It seems very controlling to me. It's more about them than you.

What I like is that Paul's very good at calming me down and coming up with practical solutions to problems. I can get in an emotional state about something and he can take me logically through the points I have to consider.

LYNDA: So he's more of a carpenter than a knight in shining armour?

LISA: Yes, exactly!

SHERRIE: First and foremost, men are brought up with the idea of being the hunter and hitting us over the head with a club and dragging us into a cave.

LYNDA: So they don't think of themselves as knights in shining armour?

SHERRIE: Men half-believe that they are knights in shining armour, but I don't think it lasts very long. They like the chase. The knight comes up on his horse. The lady in the box says, 'No, no, my Lord, not today.' 'Oh, but please!' he begs. She throws him a handkerchief and he picks it up. 'All right, then,' she says. At this, his whole demeanour changes. 'Now I've got you, I don't want you anymore,' he says. 'I only wanted to be galloping up on a horse.'

I think this happens a lot. The thrill of the chase is wonderful and nothing is ever as good afterwards.

Sport, cars, gadgets: should you show an interest or is it better just to leave them to it?

LISA: Not interested!

COLEEN: I think you should at least try to show an interest in their hobbies and passions, whether it's golf, fishing or Ray with his guitar. It's good to have your individual hobbies and passions, but you should also have joint ones. If you say, 'Oh,

Yvonne had initially been excited when Gav said he wanted to take her back to his place for the first time because he had something to show her . . .

I hate this, I hate that; I'm not interested,' then that's when you drift apart. You have nothing to talk about, because you're not interested in the same things.

LISA: I should say that Paul's not into gadgets and fast cars, but if he were, I'd go with it. It might be fun.

COLEEN: The great thing is that it doesn't matter that I'm a crap cook, because I love *Top Gear* and I love football!

DENISE: Can you speak knowledgeably about football?

COLEEN: Quite knowledgeably, but I always feel as if I sound stupid when I'm in a roomful of men. I think they think, shut up! You're a woman! Sometimes when I hear women rattling on about football, I want them to shut up, too. It's like men talking about netball! Anyway, I can't name every player in the Premier League, like my son can. Is that a male brain thing, or just that men actually care? I suppose it can't really be a male brain thing, because Gabby Logan knows her stuff, as does Helen Chamberlain, who does *Soccer AM*. She is brilliant.

DENISE: I was never interested in cars, but I've just done the medical for my HGV lorry licence! I realise that's a complete contradiction. It was triggered by something I said in all innocence on *Loose Women*. It was an episode about how you react when people say to you, 'You can't do that! You won't be able to!" Does it immediately make you want to do it?

'No not really,' I said, when it came to my turn to speak. 'If somebody says to me, "You will never be a circus trapeze artist," it wouldn't make me go out and enroll in circus school. But when Tim says, "You are the worst driver in the world. You would never pass your HGV licence," it makes me think that I might just do my HGV license and surprise him.'

The background to this is that Tim had to pass his Class 2 licence years ago, in order to drive a bin wagon in the series *Common as Muck*. Ever since, it's almost as if he has letters after his name and he thinks he is qualified to tell me that I'm a rubbish driver.

Well, I have a friend called Gary who runs a lorry driving training centre, would you believe? I didn't even know that was his job, because I know him through the Gem Appeal charity. 'Oh, the calls we've had asking if you're doing your HGV licence!' he told me. 'You've got to do it now!' So I thought, 'Right. I'm going to do it!' So I did my medical and now I'm awaiting my provisional licence.

COLEEN: Have you ever wanted to drive really fast?

DENISE: No, but my licence proves otherwise. When they were checking it for my medical, they asked, 'Do you drive a Formula One vehicle? You seem to have a lot of speeding offences on your licence.'

It's all for driving at 45 mph in a 30 mph zone, which is not something I'm proud of, but it's not as if I'm some kind of speed demon bombing down the motorway.

SHERRIE: Could you watch a whole episode of *Top Gear*?

DENISE: No, but that's partly because of Jeremy Clarkson!

How wide is the gap between men and women when it comes to romance?

COLEEN: Over the years, Ray and I have met half way, because he's become more aware of my need for romance, but sometimes I know that he's forcing it, because he doesn't get it. He's thinking, this is so ridiculous! There's nothing you can do about that, though!

I texted him when I got off the train in London the other day, 'Arrived safely. Missing you so much already and I've only just got here!'

'Yeah, cos you're an idiot!' he texted back.

I had to laugh. 'Cheers!' I texted back.

Later on I told him, 'What you need to be careful of is the day I'm not thinking that, and that might be the day it's too late!' It's not a big deal, really, it just made me laugh to see our different attitudes so clearly.

Then, on my last birthday, he threw the most amazing surprise party for me. I had no idea until it happened. It must have taken so much organising! He gave me a beautiful card and all the romantic things I love. I was bowled over, because he's usually not demonstrative like that. It threw me, because I realised that he actually is very romantic and thoughtful. He's a contradiction and I kind of like it.

LISA: Funny, that, because I think Paul is more romantic than I am.

ANDREA: Lucky you! Have you ever found a man who is compatible with you romantically, Zoe?

ZOE: I haven't, probably because I am the most romantic, stupid, soppy person in a relationship and I expect what I give and never get it back. I'm the kind of person who puts little letters under the pillow and all of that. Having said that, years ago I did wake up and come downstairs to a little love message. He had opened a bag of carrots and written, 'I love you,' in carrots! But, underneath, he should have written in raisins, 'Don't you dare look at anyone else for the rest of your life!' Still, it was very sweet.

ANDREA: Have you had any special Valentine's Days?

LYNDA: Don't fall for it! It's all a load of codswallop! If you really love somebody, why wait for one day in the year to buy a card with a printed love message and a plumped-up heart on it?

ZOE: I love Valentine's Day! It's one day a year when you can show each other that you love each other and appreciate each other, because it's so easy to forget.

LYNDA: People should be doing it every day.

ZOE: But they don't!

LYNDA: Unfortunately, I don't live up to Mr Spain, who is very romantic. He doesn't write very well, because he's dyslexic and it comes out a bit funny, but good luck to him. It doesn't mean that I love him less. Just because someone can write a romantic poem doesn't mean they actually really care.

LISA: Also, if someone is telling you they love you in letters and poems every day, it can be a bit annoying, I think. Paul and I are completely compatible romantically. We're both a bit rubbish. We were both quite romantic when we first met and now we're not at all.

ZOE: It wears off, doesn't it?

LISA: It wears off a little bit. We do the odd romantic thing. He's a good artist, so he'll put a little drawing of me in my diary, with an arrow saying, 'Have a lovely day. I love you, Nobby.' (My nickname's Nobby; don't ask why!)

From time to time, I ring him to say, like Stevie Wonder, 'I just called to say I love you.' But most of the time, we're too busy.

ZOE: Don't talk rubbish! You're never too busy. I bet you're romantic, Andrea.

ANDREA: That's why I think that Valentine's Day has a point, because it's one day a year when you're allowed to put your busyness to one side and be romantic. No one's forcing you to, though.

LISA: But they are forcing you to spend over-the-odds for dinner and you get a £5 rose for £20.

ANDREA: Or you could get a takeaway and sit and home and watch telly, but you could be romantic with it.

LISA: Or you could sit in a restaurant with a load of other soppy couples all gawping at each other. And you sit there looking at your old man, thinking, Why aren't you looking at me the way that man over there is looking at her?

ZOE: You and Lynda sound like you've got really romantic men, and you know what? You don't deserve them. I'll have them! Send them my way.

ANDREA: Interestingly, marriage therapist Andrew G. Marshall advises that to keep the romance alive, if you kiss with your eyes open . . .

LISA: . . . you can see where you're going!

ANDREA: Apparently, it's more intimate and it will re-ignite that passion.

ZOE: I think kissing with your eyes open is quite erotic, really – as long as it doesn't look like you're double-checking that you're kissing the right person!

LYNDA: Excuse me, though – as you get slightly more mature and the eyes fail, the closer you get, you go boss-eyed!

LISA: And sometimes, you don't want to see what you're kissing, do you?

ZOE: Really?

LISA: Well, sometimes. And if you've got your eyes closed, you could be with anybody!

LYNDA: Mind you, you've got to keep kissing going. I may not sound romantic, but I think kissing is very important.

ZOE: You're a snogger, aren't you?

LYNDA: No, kissing! It's got to be there. Don't forget to kiss the old man, because he loves a bit of a kiss.

LISA: Actually, we have said to each other that we need to remember to kiss more.

ANDREA: I agree, because it's one thing you can forget. You can give them lots of pecks hello and goodbye, but there's nothing nicer than having a snog thrust upon you when you're in the middle of cooking, if you know what I mean, in the nicest possible way.

LISA: You know when you were younger and you were still learning how to do it, you'd kiss with your eyes slightly open because you were looking to see if they had their eyes open?

LYNDA: Yes, and then they caught you looking, and you shut your eyes and they shut their eyes!

ANDREA: I remember my first proper snog just went on for so long that in the end I opened my eyes, thinking, how much longer do I have to stand here? Will I look silly if I pull away and run?

LISA: At least you didn't nod off.

ANDREA: No, not like I do now! (I don't mean that!)

LISA: Anything to add, Coleen?

COLEEN: Well, it often makes me laugh how typically male and female Ray and I are in our thought processes. At the moment, my son is mad about his girlfriend. She's at college in Tring and we live in Manchester, so distance is a problem. They're seventeen and very loved up. Ray gets exasperated with it. 'For God's sake, Jake, it's not like you're going to be with her forever!' he says. 'Why don't you just dump her now and get over it, because it's too painful being apart. You may as well get rid of her, because you won't be together in another six months!'

'Shut up!' I say. 'They might be!'

'Ridiculous,' he mumbles under his breath.

'Will you leave them alone!' I say.

'You love each other. I'm a great believer in fate: if you're meant to be together, you will be.' Ray says, 'They probably won't be together by the end of next week.' He's so matter-of-fact!

He accuses me of being soppy, but I say, 'No, I just want everything to be like a film.' I still do. I'm so romantic.

'But life isn't like a film,' he says.

'It could be, if two people want it to be!' I retort, although to be fair, I wouldn't want to turn into Doris Day and sing round the kitchen, wearing gingham.

He may be right about Jake's relationship and perhaps it won't last, but you don't think that when you're going through it and I certainly can't say anything like that to Jake. I was certain that my first relationship was for life. I made it to nineteen with him and it probably would have been life for me, if he hadn't have run off with someone. What's more, one of my best friends has been with her husband since they were thirteen; they're my age now and they're still just as mad about each other as they ever were. It's very rare, but it can happen. You can't turn round and say, 'Look, you're probably not going to be together next week!' It's not very nice, is it?

Do men understand female mood swings?

DENISE: No, but they have to learn to deal with them. I don't think men will ever understand. How can they? They don't have the hormonal changes that we do. It's a little bit black and white in their world, which maybe makes their lives much easier, because their moods are much more stable. But I still wouldn't want to be a man, not for a gold clock.

SHERRIE: Do women understand their own mood swings?

DENISE: I think it is something you have to go with.

SHERRIE: I didn't have mood swings with the menopause, but I had really bad sweats, which didn't depress me, but I didn't know how to cope. Nobody sat me down and said, 'This is what's going on.' I should have gone for help, but I was not a person that asked for help. I would be now, though.

Is the male midlife crisis different to the female midlife crisis?

LYNDA: With men, it will often come out in one moment of madness: 'Oh my God, I must have sex with a nineteen-year-old bird!'

With women, it will often tend to be a slower burn: 'I need a facelift. I need my breasts doing.' But women often don't have time for a midlife crisis, because they're too busy being needed by children, or elderly parents.

COLEEN: I'm not sure it does differ that much: don't women also want a toyboy and get the urge to go clubbing when they feel old? I don't know, because I've not met many women having a midlife crisis; I'm only basing it on Carol and Denise!

When she turned fifty, Carol was saying that she wanted to go to Ibiza and rave until seven in the morning. If she wasn't with Mark, that's probably what she would have done, because she doesn't feel she's experienced that kind of thing. 'Midlife crisis, or what?' I said to her. 'Yeah, I wanna get down with the kids,' she said.

Ibiza! As I pointed out, she would have been able to give birth to everyone in the club!

SHERRIE: Men don't admit it when they're having a midlife crisis. But as a newspaper recently pointed out, it's called 'men-o-pause' and it also affects men.

Actually, I was with a fifty-two-year-old the other day and I noticed that he was bright red. 'Have you just been on a sun bed?' I asked.

'No, I've just got out of the car.'

'But you're bright red.'

'I know,' he said, looking down. 'Don't tell anybody, but this keeps happening. What do you think it is?'

'It's the blooming menopause,' I said, only half-joking.

'It's not!'

'Are you hot?' I asked.

He nodded. 'I'm boiling.'

'Well, it's freezing,' I said. 'You need to see somebody.'

'What for?'

'Because they will give you something.'

'What for?' He wouldn't have it. He was so embarrassed that he got in his car and went home.

I think men have most of the same anxieties as women do about getting older, but they do seem to have more of a difficulty with sex than women. I'm assuming that's why Viagra was invented. But both sexes feel a pressure to look young and men have that same body dysmorphic thing, which is why a lot of them are now having Botox and fillers alongside women. The idea of having stuff done to your face has opened up so much in the last ten years that men are saying, 'Why can't we do it too? Why is it OK for you and not for us?' I think that is a good thing.

ANDREA: So you think it's fairly similar in men and women, Sherrie?

SHERRIE: It is and it isn't. Women tend to hide themselves during their midlife crisis; it would probably be much better for them to go out and get a twenty-seven-year-old boyfriend.

How fantastic! Go and do that, I say. Instead of embracing it, they collapse a bit and along comes the paranoia. Oh my God, what's going to happen to me?

I can understand because I had a really bad menopause, sweats like you have never seen. I'd just be sitting somewhere and suddenly I'd go bright red and pour with water, as if I'd turned on a tap of water at the top of my head. It started in 1993 and I still get it slightly at night, so it has gone on forever.

It was very hard and I think I went slightly mad for a while. I often thought that my mattress was on fire and the bed was burning my back. My skin would be boiling all over and I'd be pouring sweat. I very rarely had an uninterrupted night. I went to have HRT, but I'm allergic to it. It caused all sorts of problems for me, so I can't take it, in any form, unfortunately.

I remember being at an awards do, wearing a taupe-coloured silk suit, and I got up to present an award unaware that my entire back was soaked, from my shoulders to my ankles. My friend pulled me down. 'You can't get up! You're completely wet,' she warned.

As I sat down, I could suddenly feel the cold and wet. It looked and felt as if somebody had poured a bucket of water on me. Someone else presented the award for me. I couldn't possibly have gone up on stage like that. It was my fault for wearing silk; I should have been prepared, because it was an everyday occurrence.

How would a man cope with getting up to find his suit was soaked through? He wouldn't, would he? I don't know how I coped, to be honest, because it was horrible.

ANDREA: You poor thing! Still, it sounds like you're pretty much over the worst now.

Are men less complex than women?

COLEEN: Yes. I think women are much more complex than men. Men are very black-and-white and we're not. I know I'm more complex. For instance, I'll ask him a question and I'll know what I want the answer to be; and when I don't get it, I'm really annoyed. 'Well, don't ask my opinion, then!' he'll say.

'But you gave me the wrong answer!'

I just think we're more emotional. We run on feelings and, in my experience, we think about the meaning of our emotions in a much deeper way. We analyse things much more.

A stupid example. We'll be watching TV and Ray will say, 'This is rubbish. Let's turn it off.' And I'll say, 'Let's watch it a bit longer, because it might get better . . .'

That's what I'm saying about black-and-white: if they don't like something, they don't do it. If they don't want to go to someone's house, they won't go. For instance, we were invited out to a birthday barbeque that clashed with one of the England games in the summer. The people who invited us were very good friends of ours and they always come to us; we never go to them.

'You've got to come; it's his birthday!' I said to Ray.

'I'm not coming on Saturday. I don't care if it's his hundredth birthday; the football is on and I want to watch it at home.'

I felt the same way as Ray about the game, but I also felt guilty. 'We can't not go,' I said.

'We'll just take them out for a lovely meal next week,' he said. 'I'm not missing the football.'

I wanted to be like him! Instead, I knew I would be the one appeasing the situation, being honest, but in a nice way.

Has the gap between men and women narrowed?

SHERRIE: As I get older, I understand more how women tick and what they need from life. A lot has changed over the last fifteen years and now many of my female friends are very similar to men. They have decided what they want from life: they don't necessarily want to get married; they do not want children; they might want to have affairs. They have businesses to run and they want to rule their own lives. People used to say, 'You don't want children? What do you mean? You don't want to get married? There must be something wrong with you.' Thank God there isn't that kind of pressure anymore.

These women are strong go-getters, powerful women. In many ways they are like men, and that's great. I don't see anything wrong with it if that's what you decide and you're happy with your life. Nobody says you have to be married with children at home to be happy, anymore. That's one of the changes for the good. But it has confused men, because these days there are strong women as well as strong men in the workplace and the boardroom.

Personally, I think it's a good thing that women can make that decision and be happy with that decision. I'm not sure it would be right for me because I am an emotional character and so I need a lot of emotion in my life. My love comes from my grandson, my daughter, my mother and my brother.

Does marriage suit men?

SHERRIE: I suggested to my father once that that maybe he shouldn't have been married. There are certain men who don't suit marriage; they should live their lives unfettered because they are not the type that can take on commitment.

Women don't live those types of lives, do we? We're different because we are more likely to have commitments to anchor us and that's our choice. Ever since I was a child I have been aware of the need for responsibility and determination, forever creating more responsibility for myself because I was so driven.

ANDREA: Do you think that your father's character, his free spiritedness, affected your choices in men?

SHERRIE: Well, when I first met my husband, he told me that he could never marry me. 'I'm not a faithful person,' he said. 'I will never be faithful. Please understand that.'

'I'll change you,' I said.

'You won't. I can't be that person.'

'Oh yes you can! I will make you into that person.'

'No, you won't. Listen to me.'

He was telling me the truth and I complicated it by insisting that I was going to change him. I married him; he didn't marry me. I booked the church. I bought his suit. I booked the cars. I invited the people. I arranged the service. I did everything. All he had to do was to turn up at the church at the allotted time, which he dutifully did when I told him to. All he had to do was say, 'I do,' and that's all he did. So he didn't marry me. I married him. I can only blame myself for what he did to me afterwards, because he warned me. He was open and honest about his shortcomings. I just chose not to believe him.

ANDREA: Don't be so hard on yourself, Sherrie. There are always two sides to a story.

SHERRIE: People used to stay in a marriage because it was their duty, not because they necessarily wanted to. They were married for a long time and seemed to be happy. But there are so many divorces these days. Does it mean that people don't fight for a relationship, because it is so easy to walk away?

I think getting married should be very hard. They say getting divorced should be difficult, but I think it's the getting married that should be the toughest. If you want to get married, you should have to fight really hard and go through all sorts of obstacles. In the end you might decide, I can't be arsed with this! You might not bother.

Getting married is a massive step, but it's just so easy. I believe that having a child with somebody is a bigger thing, but a lot of people think marriage is. Lisa is not married and she believes that having a baby together is a total commitment to the relationship. I agree. Carol believes that getting married is the big commitment. Perhaps both are equally as important.

When I got married, I just wanted a white dress, a party, a big day and me at the centre of it all. 'Look at me! Look at my ring!' But when it's over and you go home, you have to get on with married life. That's the struggle. It certainly was for me. The fairy story ended a few years later and reality set in. Your husband has to be so much more than a husband. He has to be a friend and a soulmate as well for you to have a chance of it lasting.

I think it was Tony Curtis who said, 'You should only be married for ten years.' After ten years, you've done it, been it, had it, drunk it, smoked it and ate it together. There is nothing left. You have had the best ten years together that you are ever going to have. So move on and have another good ten years with somebody else.

ANDREA: That sounds like a great plan for some people I know! (Mentioning no names!)

Why don't men go to the loo together?

DENISE: Well, they do really – they all wee together when they're in the urinals! I don't know how they wee in front of each other like that!

Actually, I hate it if I'm sat having dinner and one of my friends says, 'Do you want to go to the toilet?' I always think, 'No, I don't!' When I want to go the toilet, I will just get up and go for a wee by myself, thank you very much. I was never that kind of girlie girl who always wanted to go the toilets together. What's the point of going together? I suppose that in the dating and flirting world, women do it to talk about people. But men never do. I think they just want to get in and out, because it stinks so much in there!

Mind you, on the odd occasion when I go to clubs, sometimes I've spent more time in the ladies with the girls, catching up with people I haven't seen for ages, than on the dance floor. It's quite gossipy and girlie in the loos, with everybody putting their make-up on. You can also strike up great conversations with strangers, and strangers are always becoming my best friends. As Tim says, 'Why don't you just have your phone number tattooed on your head? It would save you the energy of giving it to so many people every time you go out. Then they can just jot it down at random.'

SHERRIE: Do you think it intimidates men when women go to the ladies together?

DENISE: Generally, men find it intimidating to see women together. They worry about what we're saying. Since they don't understand women very well, they never quite know what we could be talking about. It makes them feel a little bit insecure; perhaps we are discussing performance or size or something – which nine times out of ten we probably are!

Do men gossip as much as women do?

SHERRIE: I don't think men gossip like women do, or share their feelings like women do. That's why *Loose Men* can't work, because if you said to a man, 'So, tell me, have you had an affair?' he would be affronted, wouldn't he? 'Well, that's what we talk about on this programme,' you would continue. In my case, I'd then say, 'I've never had an affair. Would I have one? Well, I don't know.' 'Don't be ridiculous!' he'd say, horrified. I don't think men can

Here we all are looking glammed-up and gorgeous

And again. Sigh! If only we always had professional hair and make-up artists on tap...
Sadly, we only look like this once a year

Some of our favourite male guests on the show...

Er, hello! Stephen Baldwin struts his stuff for Coleen;
Keith Lemon attempts to straddle the *Loose Women* panel;
Ahem. Yes, well this is a frankly gratuitous shot of a fine young specimen
we had on the show. Just because he's gorgeous!;
Denise reveals her secret weapon for seducing football-mad Russell Brand

Us girls with some of our favourite Christmas presents;
Cor blimey guv'nor, Larry Lamb is a silver fox!;
Any excuse, eh? Coleen and our handsome helper
with the blanket we made to celebrate Carol's 50th;
Coleen charms Gino D'Acampo

Coleen with her husband Ray and gorgeous daughter Ciara

Denise with Tim Healy

Lynda and Mr Spain,
somewhere hot and
sunny of course!

Lisa and her
partner Paul

Sherrie's adorable grandson Oliver (trying on his nan's glasses!) – the main man in her life!

Sherrie, Oliver and her lovely daughter Keeley

Here we are with Francis Rossi from Status Quo, he rocked our world!;
Sherrie stuns Boyzone singers Ronan Keating and Shane Lynch;
and with *Glee's* Mr Schu, actor Matthew Morrison

Start spreading the news… Carol and
Lynda put their best feet forward

The Loose Women hit the red carpet.
Watch out boys, here we come!

put it out there like we do. That's one of the big differences between men and woman, isn't it? We give out and they hold back.

DENISE: Men don't gossip? Have you met Eamonn Holmes? Eamonn is the biggest gossip I know.

SHERRIE: But what do men gossip about, then?

DENISE: You don't hear men bitching about people very much, or not in the obvious way that maybe women would. They don't care about the trivia of life; Tim just glazes over! He has no interest in celebrity or in people who he doesn't know. He cannot understand why I'd be remotely interested in some of the things or the people that fascinate me, when I don't know them. But I have a couple of straight male friends who are as into gossip and putting their nose into other people's business as I am. Obviously one's gay friends are, but I've got a couple of straight friends who are almost like gay friends in their love of gossip.

When men cry . . .

LYNDA: I have never forgotten an incident that took place when I had just left drama school and was starting out on my professional career. I was at home for a few days and one evening, from the top of the stairs, I heard talking in the kitchen. As I came down, I realised that it was my father crying. I was devastated and panic struck me, because if somebody like my father was crying, then things were really bad.

It turned out that our farm was going to be eaten up by runway number three of the proposed Wycombe Airport. All we would be left with was a house at the edge of the runway, so Dad felt that his only option was to go into contracting out farm equipment, like combine harvesters and tractors. However, in order to do this, he had to buy the machinery – and a combine harvester was probably the same price as a Rolls Royce.

As I listened outside the kitchen door, I heard Dad saying tearfully to my mum, 'We just don't have enough money! The numbers don't add up and I don't know what we're going to do. If I could just get the money to buy one combine harvester to rent out, that would be all we need to get started.'

Shortly after this, I got a part in the telly series, *General Hospital*, and I gave Dad the first £500 I earned, which helped towards buying his first combine harvester. I was so grateful to be able to pay him back in a small way for everything that he and my mum had done for me. It got him off the ground.

COLEEN: What a wonderful thing to be able to do!

LYNDA: After that, I really only saw him cry at the end of his life, when mum got Alzheimer's. Her illness was devastating for him in so many ways. One of the worst times was when we took her to the home and she asked my dad, 'Why are you doing this to me? I thought you loved me. I would never have put you in a home.' My dad had tears streaming down his face. He felt he had failed her, even though he couldn't look after her properly after breaking his neck. She had fallen over and broken her hip, so she not only had Alzheimer's, but was also disabled. Still he said, 'I've let her down.' That was terrible for him.

He died very suddenly and unexpectedly, when we were expecting mum to die. I think he was just so physically weary, and emotionally exhausted by going to visit her and being confronted with the fact that there was nothing left of who she had been. I think he just gave up.

COLEEN: That's so sad, love. I know that was a very tough time for you.

DENISE: Yes, I don't know how you got through it. You're such a survivor, Lynda. What about you, Coleen? Do the men in your life cry?

COLEEN: Apart from welling up at Ciara's sports day, Ray only cries out of genuine sadness, if someone dies or someone close to him is hurt. But if we have a row, I won't find him crying in the corner. He is a stoical Yorkshire man. If I saw him crying because he was upset, it would absolutely kill me.

It really upsets me when I see men cry. Having said that, I once had a boyfriend who cried more than me. The first couple of times, I thought, aw, he's so sensitive and soft. Then a year down the line I thought, no, he's just a drip! It was very unattractive. He cried at everything. He cried if we had a row, so I became the man, saying, 'Come on, I didn't mean it!' I didn't like that. He was a real mummy's boy. As you can see, I've been from one extreme to the other many times when it comes to men, always thinking I liked the other end of the spectrum.

I hate crying myself. I really try not to do it in front of

people, including my husband. I don't want sympathy and I hate women who use tears as a weapon. There are women or girls out there who will cry at the drop of a hat, but I think, oh don't do the tears thing! I can't bear it.

If I've ended up crying during a row, I've often said to Ray, 'And I'm not crying because I'm upset, I'm crying because I'm really angry and I hate you!' I wouldn't want him to think I was crying because I was really devastated! I'm crying because I want to punch his lights out. The tears come out of anger.

Very occasionally, if something is really bad, I'll cry in front of somebody. In that case, they will know that it's serious. It used to worry Ray that I wouldn't cry in front of anyone. When my mum died, I didn't cry, because I felt I had to be strong for the kids. There's nothing worse than seeing your mother cry.

I saw my mum cry with frustration now and again, when she'd got to the end of her tether with eight kids and none of the luxuries we have. I don't know how she managed. But it would be over as soon as it started. I never saw her sitting there hurting and crying and I never once saw my father cry.

LISA: When my nan died, I ended up organising the funeral, which hijacked my grief to a degree. I had to keep it together, partly because of Beau. Like you, Coleen, I wanted to be strong for her on the day. She didn't cry because I didn't cry, but she cried later that night and was upset with herself for crying, because I'd been so strong at the funeral and she felt she should be, too. 'No, you absolutely shouldn't,' I assured her. So we managed to address that and hopefully she's got her grief in a place where she can understand it.

Paul knows all about bereavement, because he lost his father in his late twenties and his sister when she was 36. He made a point of making me go on long walks after the funeral, which meant that I couldn't hide from my grief by being busy. So I was confronted with it and eventually I hit a wall. There were a couple of days when I couldn't stop crying.

COLEEN: Crying can be healthy, as long as it doesn't get out of control.

When my marriage to Shane was breaking up, I didn't cry in front of anyone because I didn't want sympathy. But I would cry on my own. Perhaps I didn't cry in front of people because I felt so out of control – and that was the only thing I could control.

There was also the feeling that people were thinking, poor her!

It was lovely of them, but I kind of wanted to say, 'Do you know what? I'm embarrassed enough and hurt and humiliated enough.' I was appalled by the thought of people patting me on the head and saying, 'You'll be all right.' So my default stance was, 'I'm fine!'

LISA: I cry at everything. Actually, that's not strictly true. I cry at the things that don't really matter. The things that really matter, because they're so immense, I daren't even start with the tears, because they'll never stop. So you'll see no tears then.

DENISE: My dad and I both cry easily. I used to ring my dad on a Sunday night and he'd be crying at Cilla Black's *Surprise Surprise,* when they reunited people at the end. He's a softie when it comes to those types of programmes.

Tim wells up at the kids' prowess. If Matthew plays him a new song and it's really good, Tim will fill up and so will I. We are all a bit prone to waterworks in our family, I suppose.

Often men can't bear women crying, can they? Is it conditioning? I don't know. We are often crying because of things they've done or said, so I suppose it's a guilt thing as well!

I hate it when I see men cry properly, partly because it's such a rare occurrence and I know something really bad's happened, especially in Tim's case. Obviously Louis cries to get his own way because he is a little drama queen, but I know when he's doing that. He's inherited that from his mother.

LISA: I don't think tears necessarily signify deeper feelings in a man or a woman. I went out with a boyfriend who behaved appallingly and cried afterwards, saying, 'I'll never do it again!' But he wasn't crying because he'd hurt me; they were the tears of self-loathing.

COLEEN: Being actors, can you just turn the tears on and off?

DENISE: I'm pretty good at it, yes. When I did *The Rise and Fall of Little Voice* at the Manchester Exchange, I had to have a breakdown in a really powerful scene at the end of the play and I was able to cry every night, because it was so well written and moving. Obviously, it requires much more effort in some roles, because the script is rubbish. You have to make something of it. It's quite painful, because you have to call upon really sad events in your life, some of which you wouldn't choose to remember.

Still, I find it easier to cry on screen than to laugh. I always find that my stage laugh is rubbish. It's just more difficult for me to recreate laughter. I do it, but when I see it, I'm never as convinced as I am when I cry on screen. Some actors do it brilliantly. Helen Worth, who plays Gail in *Corrie*, is a fantastic laugher. Unfortunately, on screen Gail rarely gets anything to laugh at! She is always great, though. Eva Pope is also a very good laugher and another really good actress.

As far as crying in real life goes, the trouble is that when you are an actress and people know you can cry in a role, there is sometimes an element of wondering if they're crocodile tears. Tim sometimes wonders, because I'm quite good at crying for my work and he knows that.

LISA: I've done some really good crying-acting to Paul after arguments – proper body racking sobs, in a corner. If I were in a drama, I would obviously be a broken woman! 'Oh, you're crying again,' he'll say. 'Try saying something.' What he actually wants from me are words that show I've registered what I've done wrong. He needs me to form a sentence that says to him, 'I really mean that I'm not going to say or do this again.' Crying is just another way of saying, 'Please come and cuddle me and make me feel better.' It's a bit of a cop-out sometimes.

The best thing I can do to convince Paul that something has impacted on me is to say nothing and do nothing, because that way, at least he knows that I've absorbed it and I'm digesting and understanding it. I'm not performing it or doing anything for effect.

Are men better at getting over break-ups?

COLEEN: I think men are better at covering up their hurt. Their pride kicks in and they put on an I'm-not-bothered face. They don't discuss it with their mates, either. Every man I've spoken to has said that. He might have one best mate that he confides in and says, 'I'm devastated.' The mate then says, 'Come on, let's go out for a drink and get pissed.' They have different ways of coping. If they do cry, it'll be on their own, crying themselves to sleep.

That's why I love being a woman. We go round to our girlfriends or they come to us and they will stay until four or five in the morning and discuss every aspect of it, however intimate it may be. I think that's healthier. The only thing is that men seem to get over it quicker than women do, because women replay and replay it, whereas men put it away, or go out and sleep with the first available woman. Their mates might say, 'Come on, let's go out on the pull.' But women are more emotional, so I think the last thing you want to do when you've just split up with someone is go straight out and be chatted up by somebody else on the same day. I can't think of anything worse. You're too heartbroken.

SHERRIE: On the same day? In the same decade, more like! Well, in my case, anyway. I'm generalising, but I would say that a man needs to be with somebody more than a woman does. Women can survive on their own. They are more stoic.

If you are stoic, you can gird your loins and get on with things. Men collapse and need someone there. They don't cope well on their own, so they move on to the next person who will look after them. After a break-up, you often hear that they have found somebody else.

DENISE: Men usually rebound straight into the arms of somebody else. They very rarely leave a relationship unless they are dumped, or have somebody else lined up. I don't think they have the confidence to stand on their own two feet as much as women do. Often women will have the strength to leave a desperately unhappy relationship and stand alone. A man would probably start an affair and leave for their lover.

I just don't think men have the balls to be on their own. It's interesting, because the men I'm thinking of can be quite high achieving; they haven't necessarily been with women who are archetypal housewives. These are men who in theory can stand on their own two feet, but in practice need to be in a relationship.

SHERRIE: Men have tunnel vision. Women have a bigger periphery. They live in a wider world. I find that I replay everything in my mind, constantly thinking how things could have been different. Carol is always going on at me to stop. 'You mustn't do it. You're wasting your time,' she tells me. Well, she can afford to say that, with a twenty-seven-year-old boyfriend, can't she?

But she's right. I've been going over and over things since 2001, when I split up with my husband. That's nine years of replay. I'm sure that my ex-husband found somebody within weeks after we broke up. I know he did, in fact, because people saw him. He always has somebody. So it's futile to keep saying, 'If only.' Just get over it!

Carol has taught me to get on with life and be happy. 'There

*'That'll teach him for not calling me!' shrieked Amanda,
as she contemplated where to stab the last needle . . .*

are no wrong decisions or bad decisions,' she always says to me. 'There are only decisions – and you live by them. You may think afterwards, actually I shouldn't have done that. But you can't go back. So you should accept that it was a decision you made there and then and move on.'

If you lived by her rules, you'd probably be a lot happier. I'm sure she doesn't always manage it, but she is right to try. Still, it doesn't stop you thinking about what might have been.

COLEEN: I worry that it's made you a bit bitter towards men, Sherrie. You shouldn't be, because there are some great men out there, some brilliant men. They're not all bad. You have to give people a chance.

OK, if they let you down, you don't speak to them again, you move on and learn from the experience, but you've been so hurt that I think you've put up this wall. I don't think you can cope with the idea of someone hurting you like that again. The thing is though, you are such a fabulous woman. I'd love to see you with someone wonderful.

SHERRIE: I know, but . . .

COLEEN: Look at Lynda! As she herself says, who would have thought that she would be getting married again on her sixtieth birthday? So you can never predict how life's going to turn out. I'm hoping that you will be like Lynda and meet someone who makes you very happy.

SHERRIE: I suppose it would be nice . . .

COLEEN: But why are you still not divorced? I would be the

opposite. Get out of my life! I'd think. I'd want the divorce through immediately. That's the way it was for me. Shane really didn't want us to get divorced and we were getting on great, so I could have said to him, 'OK, we'll leave it until I meet someone.' But I had to draw that line under our relationship, so that I could move on.

SHERRIE: The reason I haven't got a divorce is laziness, really.

COLEEN: Is it? Well, let me just say that my divorce was really important to me and I think that if you got the divorce through, you'd find it much easier to move on. You were saying the other day that you don't know who you are now. When you fill in forms, you still have to tick the 'married' box. And yet you're not married. How can you move on, then? How can you end it properly?

If you do meet someone, how are they going to feel? You'll say all these terrible things about your marriage and he'll ask, 'So when did you get divorced?' And you'll have to tell him, 'I'm not.' If I was a bloke, I'd think, Uh-oh! Why not?

It frustrates me, because I think you can move on further than you have. If you get a divorce you'll straightaway feel, I'm an independent woman. I am my own boss. He's gone.

SHERRIE: It's sad that I haven't found anybody else in the nine years since I split up with my ex-husband and you're right that it's because I've put up a massive barrier, not to protect me from men so much, as to protect me from emotional hurt and pain. My heart was broken so badly that I feel I couldn't possibly take the risk of it being broken again. I don't think I would survive it. I still feel weary and emotionally beaten. I'm very cautious and find it hard to trust anyone. But that doesn't mean that I don't love men. They are fabulous.

I love looking at the Robert Redfords and the Cary Grants of this world. I'm sure neither of them were much like the way they appear in films, but it doesn't matter to me. I just let my imagination go and enjoy them aesthetically. There is no one more gorgeous than Robert Redford in *The Sting*. That glorious boy with his beautiful eyes! It is sexiness beyond belief.

Sometimes reality is too stark and too painful to bear, with too many doubts and memories, which is why I love going into my own world. I'll never get over the pain of my marriage split; twenty-six years is too long to get over.

The only time it was good was when we first met. I should have believed him when he told me that he wasn't the person I wanted him to be. Sadly, I wasn't happy for quite a long time and neither was he, I'm sure. That's wasted two lives. But at least I had Keeley.

If I'd walked away in 1984, when I had Keeley, perhaps we would both have gone on to live happy separate lives. That's why I'm always mulling over the past and I can't forgive myself for not acting when I should have. But, as Carol says, you have to accept that you do things in life for whatever reason.

COLEEN: What was it that broke your heart so badly, Sherrie?

SHERRIE: I think it was the feeling that the fairy story had been smashed. The image of the little girl who wanted to be married and have a baby disintegrated. Cinderella lived happily ever after, but I didn't. The idyll shattered into terrible pain and sadness for everybody. That's what I couldn't forgive.

Having said that, I'm finally trying to move on, because I have spent nine years ruminating and going over it and replaying it in my mind. Any more time would be a real waste of life! I had to understand what had happened, after twenty-six years, though. I needed to work it out and come to accept it. Now it's time to say, 'Right, I've got however many years left, so let's have a ball. Let's have a good time – and you never know, I might meet somebody.'

COLEEN: I really hope you do, because you're so fabulous.

LYNDA: There are lots of women in England on their first or second divorce; when you get to your fifties, you are very conscious that if you don't get on with your life now, it is going to pass you by. So you need to re-evaluate. Where will you go? How will you get out there?

I think doing voluntary work can be very fulfilling and it gets you out there too. At a recent volunteer's charity awards, I saw a man who had been made redundant and now takes kids to school when their parents can't cope. One of the girls he helped was interviewed and she told us that she could talk to him without embarrassment, that she had stopped playing truant and that 'he has made my mum come home at tea time.' That's the kind of voluntary work anybody can do and it makes a huge difference to your own life and to the life of the person you're helping.

Alzheimer's cafes are really interesting. They are cafes

set up by the Alzheimer's Society, where volunteers can turn up and sit with someone for a couple of hours and play chess or read to them. It gives such pleasure to the person with Alzheimer's and although it's unlikely that you'll meet the man of your dreams there, who knows what can happen on the bus there? It gets you out of the house and keeps you active and interacting. The more you get out there and talk, the more chance you have of something happening. When someone asks you that evening if you've done anything interesting in the day, you'll have something to talk about.

LISA: You've definitely got to get out there, I agree. But to go back to the original question, I don't think men are better at getting over break-ups, as it happens. Maybe we hurt in different ways and I don't know if getting over it more quickly means that you're better at dealing with it.

I think men are more logical about break-ups. Women, sometimes coming from a more emotional place, will spend days and days analysing what went wrong, whereas blokes tend not to overanalyse things. So they might come to a conclusion much more quickly and succinctly.

But men are insecure and they are aware of their own shortcomings. They do beat themselves up about things that perhaps they could have done differently. So I don't think you can say categorically that men cope better with break-ups.

Is it more acceptable for a man to get blind drunk than for a woman?

COLEEN: I can see a man in the gutter lying in his own vomit after having too much to drink and I think, 'Oh, blokes! Men!' I see a woman of the same age in the same situation and I think she looks absolutely revolting. When women say, 'If men can do it, why can't we?' I want to say, 'Why do you want to?' It's almost accepted that men can be pigs, but women are nicer than that. If that's what being a man is, I don't want to be one, thanks!

Carol and I are always arguing about this on *Loose Women*. She says, 'So men can binge drink and women can't?' Well, I'd rather neither did, but I tut and think, what an idiot! when it's a bloke, whereas when it's a girl, lying in the gutter with her skirt around her ears, it's vile. Don't get me wrong, I love men; I adore them. But women are *lovely*. I would rather men put us on a pedestal and thought, aren't women beautiful? I've never wanted to be one of the lads.

LISA: I'm just about OK with the face down in the gutter bit; it's the skirt around her ears that worries me! There's something really undignified about it, not to mention vulnerable. I know that if you're drunk, you'd really rather your toilet parts weren't on show. If you were sober and you could make the choice, you wouldn't do that!

Former First Lady Laura Bush has spoken for the first time about her husband's drinking habits, telling a US magazine, 'When he'd poured enough drink, he could be such a bore. I didn't think it was funny in the end.' Has she got a point? So are you tolerant of booze bores and do you change when you're under the influence?

JANE: Having a drink relaxes you a little bit, but a lot of people don't have that switch-off, which is a dangerous thing. There are booze bores and there are people who have a really good time. We all know people who are nasty with alcohol and people who aren't.

My other half was teetotal for about twelve years. When you've got someone who doesn't drink, while you're having a glass of wine and getting into the mood, and they say, 'Can we go now?' you kind of wish they would have a drink, because you want them to enjoy the night.

KATE: That's another kind of booze bore, isn't it?

JANE: So he has the odd glass of wine now.

COLEEN: Have you turned him to drink?

JANE: Yes, I've turned him to drink! Well, he's not getting fed, is he? 'They ate better on *Tenko*,' he said the other day, and he's right!

KATE: So he's in that shed, like Sue Ellen! Glug!

JANE: He'll be doing the home brew next! I can feel it coming on . . .

KATE: So you just get him drunk now.

JANE: And then he'll eat anything! But I'm glad he's now having the odd glass of wine, because he's a lot more sociable now and not so shy. But for a lot of people alcohol is not a good thing, because they don't have that switch-off, as I said.

SHERRIE: I used to have a fear of alcohol. The idea of drinking too much frightened me. It was partly because I used to get very bad hangovers, like migraine hangovers, and also because, many years ago, I used to drink too much, when things were bad in my relationship. Fortunately the hangovers were so bad that I don't drink too much now. I lose a day, or two days, and I can't bear the pain. But a little alcohol can relax you. It's always funny when Col and I go out with the girls, because at the end of the night they'll be on the floor and we'll be having a pot of tea.

KATE: I'm with you girls – and Jane's the same. We don't get drunk, do we? We might have a nice warm glow about us, but you've never seen me drunk, have you, Coleen?

COLEEN: No . . .

KATE: Carol keeps saying to me, 'You should, you'd be more interesting!'

COLEEN: I think that's where drunks become boring. Because they're getting drunker and drunker, they don't realise that you've been the same since you got there and you've all got on great. Then they say, 'Look at you, you're so boring!' I want to say, 'No, you are, because you've just said that for the 150,000th time!

KATE: Repeat!

COLEEN: Repeating themselves! My husband definitely does not have that cut-off point, but I have. When I went out last Saturday, I had a few wines and I got very merry and had that lovely tipsy feeling; then I stopped, because I thought, I don't want to go to that next level of feeling awful or being sick. But sometimes Ray cannot stop. He has to go on all night, which is really boring and really unattractive. Even worse, they think they're attractive, but don't even think about it when you get home!

KATE: They think they're interesting as well! 3a.m. is when you think, the evening is done. Basically, anything that happens after 3a.m. is just a repeat of what happened before, except that they think it's more fascinating and it's less audible.

SHERRIE: I turn into Looby Lou when I've had a few drinks. Mind you, you wouldn't know the difference!

KATE: I was going to say that!

Is it more acceptable for men to get angry?

SHERRIE: I think it's very scary when women lose their tempers. Only because when they do, there is usually much more behind it than just having a good old row. Men are quite simple creatures, aren't they? They have an argument and it's boom-boom-boom, but women are so taken up with everything else at once.

With me, I could actually lift a car and throw it when I'm angry. There is much more going on with women when they lose their tempers. I know men are very physical and stronger than we are, but I'm talking more about the mental side of things. So it frightens me when women lose their tempers.

LISA: I find it the opposite, actually. I think that generally women are a lot more emotive and more open about their feelings. So I would find it a lot easier to handle a woman getting in a rage or in a state or being aggressive than I would a man. I think there is nothing scarier than a bloke who is angry with you, because of the physical presence and aggression. I have been on the receiving end of male bullying and there is nothing more terrifying, especially in the workplace, for example. I find it far worse.

ANDREA: This came up because of something Janet Street Porter said and I think what she was touching on is that sometimes a woman loses control. I'm not saying all women are like this, but sometimes perhaps, when a woman loses her temper, she is not just arguing with you about this point here. She's going to bring up what you did six months ago and a year ago. 'And by the way you did this too!' Do you feel a woman is more likely to lose control when she gets angry?

SHERRIE: Yes, because when I lose my temper, I have a red mist. I can't control it and bring it back. That's what I mean about being scary.

ZOE: Yes, I think that when we go, we go. I'm very, very calm in life, but when I lose my temper, I lose it quite badly. But I'm not intimidated by men and their temper, because I'm used to it. I've experienced it a lot over the years. However, I think I'd react differently to a woman losing her temper with me. I'd say, 'Why are you getting angry?'

The other day, a man in the street lost his temper with me, because my dog ran off. It was, like, pathetic, because he was obviously in a very bad mood and flew off the handle with me. My reaction was to be angry back and say, 'Don't you talk to me like that!' I lost it. But perhaps I wouldn't have reacted in the same way to a woman. Maybe I would have calmed the situation. Still, everybody gets angry and it's OK to get angry. As long as it's not physical, I think it's OK to express anger.

ANDREA: What do you make of Janet's argument that it's rather more frowned upon for a woman to lose her temper in public? Do you worry about losing your temper? How you are seen?

LISA: I hate it when I lose my temper. I think when a woman loses her temper, it can be really ugly. I hate myself when I lose my temper – and I do have a temper. When Paul and I argue, I sometimes get properly really cross and I never want him to see me like that and I certainly never want my daughter to see me angry like that. I think it shows weakness if you totally lose it.

ZOE: I don't think there is any difference between a man losing his temper and a woman losing hers and I don't think you should hate yourself for losing your temper. In an ideal world, nobody should lose it: it is exhausting and it causes so much upheaval. But it happens, and I don't think it makes any difference whether it's a woman or a man.

ANDREA: Does society see it as less ladylike for a woman to lose her temper?

SHERRIE: To say it's frowned upon seems very old fashioned. I haven't heard that for years. I don't think it matters. As you said, Zoe, as long as nobody gets hurt . . .

LISA: I've seen some men rant and rave, irrespective of whether you are in the room or not. It gets to the point when it doesn't even matter if you are there. I think it's the same with both sexes. We all give as good as we get.

Can good friends go on to become partners?

LISA: I've never done it. I'd like to think that I could fall in love with someone for all those right reasons, but I'm a bit too superficial! For me, it's the initial look of somebody and the spark that happens when you don't know someone. I love the fact that you don't know, and the danger and excitement that goes with that.

I love the development and the unravelling and finding out that you're actually quite compatible! It's really exciting to discover that. Sometimes you can recognise that immediately. I did when I met Paul. I knew as soon as I met him that he was absolutely my type and really special. I moved in with him three weeks later. Is there that same excitement when you get together with a friend?

COLEEN: I think it's lovely if it happens. It usually happens for a reason, as in they've helped each other through a bad situation or relationship and then all of a sudden they get closer and closer. But I would find it very strange, I think. And I would be so frustrated that we'd wasted all those years of not being together!

When my marriage split up, some of the friends that Shane and I had known for years started asking me out. It was bizarre. I couldn't be friends with them after they asked me out, because suddenly there was an awkwardness. Some of them were people who had come round to the house when Shane wasn't in and I had gladly sat and chatted with them, or they had stayed overnight while he was away and it hadn't occurred to me that they might fancy me. Then as soon as we split up, they would ring up and say something like, 'Do you fancy going out for lunch?'

I remember this happening one time in particular and, being naive, I said to my sister, 'He's been a friend for something like twenty years. Maybe he really is just asking me out to lunch.'

'Has he asked you out to lunch in those twenty years?' she asked.

'No!'

'He's not just asking you out to lunch then, is he? Otherwise he'd have done it before.'

Of course, then you think, oh my God, I can't be friends with you now!

DENISE: I know it happens, because I often read about it, but to be honest it always baffles me when people say, 'We'd been friends for eight years and then we just looked at each other in a different way.' I can understand it if there has been something keeping you apart, like other attachments, but quite how a sexual attraction suddenly emerges after eight years, I don't really know. Attraction is usually instantaneous, isn't it? It certainly has been with me. I've always known what I wanted – or didn't want – straight away, and if there's a spark but nothing happens immediately, it fizzles.

Mind you, many times, with my beer goggles on, I've thought, 'I could . . .' My friend Philip calls it the mystery bus. He has observed that you can be in a room of people who aren't remotely attractive, but after a few sherbets, you come back from the toilet and suddenly everybody is beautiful, because the mystery bus has been and dropped people off. He always used to say, 'Oh no, I've got a date tomorrow. I'm sure it will somebody off the mystery bus.'

LYNDA: That's funny! I remember that happening to me, too. But look, I think this has to do with people's understanding of what a relationship is, how sexual it is. I would never be friends for years and then suddenly develop an attraction because I just don't see relationships that way. What is the point of having a relationship without sex? Certainly I can't have a relationship that doesn't have a physical side; I can't conceive of a relationship that doesn't always have sex in it. I mean I know it comes and goes, but God forbid that the sex should ever go out of my marriage, because it's a big part of it. I don't think it ever sounds right when people say, 'We've been married for twenty years and we don't have sex anymore.' Lots of people seem to give it up before they should.

If they're not careful, some women adopt the no-sex vibe after they have brought up their children, which is why we have ageism. There's a sense that somehow, if you are no longer of childbearing age, then you are of no interest to men. It's such rubbish.

Can you remain friends after a break-up?

COLEEN: I can understand it if you've experienced something together and you still get on well, but you're no longer in love and you no longer even fancy each other. But I also understand why it can be difficult for new partners to accept that you're still friends with an ex. I don't know how I'd feel if Ray was best friends with someone he'd been together with for years, especially since I work away a lot. If I rang up from London and he said that she was round, I'm not sure I'd be totally happy about it. But I do think it's possible to be good friends.

Shane and I are not on the phone every minute of the day; we don't see each other all the time, but we're still friends and we can have a laugh. Ray's cool with that. He knows we've got a history together and, of course, the kids.

I've bumped into ex-boyfriends and been delighted to see them. It's not a case of, oh no, I'd better not speak to him because I've got a past with him. Likewise, I like hearing about Ray's past and I've met ex-girlfriends of his and even people he's just spent a night with. I'm fine about it. That's all part of life. I'm his future and they're his past. As long as you don't feel threatened or make someone feel threatened by it, I think it can work.

DENISE: It depends on the break-up. Obviously some people have acrimonious splits and so it's understandable that they don't want to be friends. But where there are children involved, you should certainly try to be friends, although it is very difficult if one person still desires the other.

I've known different people to have very different reactions: some who have broken up with their children's father absolutely hate their ex's guts and others who have found that they are better friends and better parents as a result of being apart.

When you first break-up with someone, I don't think you can go straight to being friends. There probably has to be a certain amount of time that lapses before you can create another relationship between the two of you. I know people who are much better friends since they split up. They were lovers for a long time, but they were never friends until they split up.

I'm friends with a lot of my ex-boyfriends from a long time ago. We all went to each other's fiftieth birthday parties. But I'm not friends with my ex-husband; I just don't see him.

LISA: I've had a relationship with someone and then become

friends afterwards. You can share so much with someone that it's a pity never to see them again. Maybe they were a massive influence on your life for a long time or maybe they knew members of your family who are no longer around. But it's a big ask to expect a new partner to accept that your ex is your friend. That's when it's complicated. It's fine if you're not attached and it's fine if your new partner is fine about it, but when they're not, that's when you have to consider whether you should cut the ties.

Of course, there has to be a balance. When you get to a certain age, you have to accept that your partner has a past and they have had partners before you. Sometimes a friendship is possible, sometimes not. I once had an ex who took enormous pleasure out of the fact that he'd been there and he made that clear to my partner at the time. That's something that only two men can pick up on.

'What's the problem?' I asked my boyfriend, when he told me he was uncomfortable about us seeing my ex.

'You don't get it, Lisa, because it's not a girl thing. It's something that goes on between two men. I can see it, he knows I can see it and I'm not comfortable.'

That's when it doesn't work, when your ex is almost enjoying the fact that he is an ex more than he is your friend.

LYNDA: I don't understand couples that split up and then stay very good friends. In my book, they can't ever have been involved passionately with each other if they can just say goodbye, yet go on seeing each other. I suppose there are always exceptions, but why would you split up after years and years if you are such good friends? If you're still having sex, then surely you still care about one another – or at least one of you cares.

Chapter 5

In the family way

'BUT I THOUGHT YOU WERE PICKING THE KIDS UP FROM SCHOOL!'

There's no denying that domesticity can be trying, especially if you're experiencing it in tandem with a man who can't even remember to put the bins out. There are more important areas of home life, of course, where the man's role is crucial, especially when it comes to fatherhood and being supportive partners to mums-to-be, but that's still no reason to forget about the blooming bins, for goodness sake!!!!

We tend to think that men aren't naturally as nurturing as women are, but sometimes the evidence contradicts us, especially when we're off bread-winning and they're stoically holding the fort. How much it matters to your bloke whether you earn more than he does can be vital to the balance of your relationship. Men are a lot better at feeling superior than the other way around, it seems! But maybe times are finally changing . . .

Being in a relationship, especially when there are kids, involves a lot of give and take. How difficult is it to find the right equilibrium (i.e. get things our own way!)? Should we beat them, join them, nag them – or just sit there with our arms crossed, dreaming about Enrique Inglesias and making a shopping list for the weekend's meals, while they drone on about cars and fishing?

On a more serious note, a long-term relationship can throw up some pretty big challenges. Infidelity, for one – and betrayal. So is fidelity all it's cracked up to be – and how would you cope if your partner was unfaithful? Hmmm, more wine, please!

Are women naturally more nurturing than men?

COLEEN: I'm always saying that men are programmed to be the hunters and women to be the nurturers, even today. I enjoy being out hunting, but I'm at my happiest when I'm at home nurturing. My natural instinct is to be at home.

My family always come first, no matter what. If I was on *Loose Women* tomorrow and I got a call to say, 'One of the kids is sick, you need to come,' I would go immediately. If my boss said, 'You can't go. We'll fire you if you do,' I'd say, 'Well, fire me. I'm going home.'

When Ray has to go away to work and I'm at home, he'll say, 'God, I'm really going to miss Ciara.' He's obsessed with our daughter, but it's not the same for him as it is for me when I'm away. He's very soft with her; if she does great things on sports day, he cries. But it's just not the same. Whether that's because we are natural nurturers, or because by carrying them in the womb we've known them nine months longer and the bond is stronger, I don't know, but it's definitely different.

When Shane accepted the part of Danny in *Grease* in Manchester, he also accepted that he would only be able to

*When Dave told Belinda he wanted to be a house-husband,
this wasn't quite what she'd had in mind . . .*

get home every Saturday night, for twenty-four hours. No amount of money would induce me to stay away all week! I would just miss the children too much, whereas it's definitely different for men. There will be men out there shaking their heads, but they're the exceptions.

LYNDA: Women probably are more nurturing generally. Often the biggest threat to a man is when a woman has a baby. People talk about postnatal depression and the effect on women of having a child, which is great, but not enough is done to help men understand that women can love and love and love; the more people they are asked to love, the more they do love. Men can't understand it. They think that if a woman loves her children deeply, she can't love her husband as much.

It's probably because, much as men love their children, they don't love them in that all-consuming way. So it's important for women to include their partners at the same time as experiencing this all-consuming love for a baby. Unfortunately, that can often mean being sexual and two months after the baby is born, you might have stitches and not feel very sexual. So many women have said to me, 'He's so selfish! It's the last thing on my mind.' 'Well, try and make it the first thing on your mind,' I've said. 'If you don't want to, just get going and your body will take over. It doesn't have to be the best sex ever, but he needs it to make him feel secure and for the good of the relationship.'

From the outside, it can easily feel excluding to look at this amazing aura of love surrounding a mother and child. Also, who is to say that seeing you breastfeeding doesn't bring something back for a man, an animal memory of his own experiences as a baby?

It's not just breastfeeding, either. I have a feeling that many men don't want to watch their partner giving birth. 'You must, if you love me!' the woman says. But if they don't really want to and afterwards they have this image in their heads that they can't dispel, it may make lovemaking that much more difficult for them.

Either way, this is the time that things start to go wrong in the bedroom in a lot of marriages. That period when the children are young and the mother is focused totally on them is bloody hard. It should be discussed more, so that it can be sorted out.

COLEEN: I definitely see women as being the nurturers. I'm horrified at any kind of child cruelty, but more horrified when there's a woman involved. That's because there's this expectation that women are nurturers. And I'm always absolutely disgusted when I read that a woman has left her husband and kids and gone off with another man. When a man does it, I write him off as a b******, but when a woman does it, I'm much more horrified. How could she leave her kids? I don't get it.

If I went off with another man, I'd have to take my children! Or at least work out a way to see them. Yet some women just walk away and don't look back. I cannot get my head round that. I always think there must be some mental illness involved, but I don't think that with a man. I just think, oh well, that's a man for you, shirking his responsibilities. Off he goes for a younger model!

And when a man says, 'Couldn't be dealing with kids; not interested,' I'll say, 'You don't know what you're missing.' But when a woman says, 'I can't stand kids. I'd hate to have kids,'

I always think there's something wrong there – and there is! There must be.

SHERRIE: Don't let Carol hear you say that!

CAROL: Women with kids always say, 'Why haven't you got any children?' Like I'm the weirdo! No, *you're* the weirdo! Why do women without children always have to justify their decision? Yet women with children never do. It does my head in.

COLEEN: Of course, there are exceptions to every rule!

Was your partner supportive when you were pregnant?

LISA: Paul was very supportive. He knew I was pregnant with Beau before I did, because I wasn't brave enough to look at the wee stick!

COLEEN: Ray loved every minute that I was pregnant. He was at every scan and doctor's appointment and wanted to feel every kick. He was there for the entire birth and he did everything for the first ten days. I didn't even change a nappy. When I had Ciara, I practically went straight back to work, so he was the main parent for the first three months. I think it hurts him that she sobs so much when I'm going away, because he does so much for her. But that bond with the mother is something so strong, isn't it?

'Don't you just love pregnancy?' beamed Alison as John frantically
made the third banana and gherkin pizza of the day.
'Yes dear – it's magical!'

When I was pregnant with Shane Junior, the first time he kicked, Shane was very excited. But after that, when I'd say, 'Quick, give me your hand, it's kicking!' he'd say, 'I felt it the first time.' Ray, on the other hand, would sit with his hand on my stomach every time I moved or sat down, because he wanted to feel every kick. So they had very different approaches, although they equally adore their children. Shane absolutely loved them, but he wasn't a hands-on dad. He never bathed them or changed their nappies. I used to say to him, 'It's easy to love them; it's the parenting that's hard.'

Ray is a fantastic advert for a stepfather. I'm not just saying it because I love him. My boys would say it too, as would my friends. You would never, ever think, she's obviously his and they're not. They're all the same.

Of course, in the first couple of years it was really hard to find the balance between being strict and loving. Ray had no experience with kids; I was in the middle. They'd have a big row and all end up not speaking to me, even if I hadn't been in the house. It was always my fault, especially if I didn't side one way or the other. 'If it had been the other way round, I think I would have walked away,' I said to Ray.

He has done wonders with the two boys. He's totally sorted them out. They could have gone one way or the other, but he was really strict with them and they always knew where the line was. They crossed it a couple of times with dire consequences and then learned never to cross it again.

He could easily have said to them, 'Do what you want. I don't really care, because you're not my kids and my life doesn't need to be this difficult.' But he totally cared and he disciplined them with love. He absolutely adores them. They've got a band and they supported us on tour – Ray watched them every night and every night he cried at the side of the stage! He was just so proud of them. One of them even wrote on his Facebook page that Ray was his inspiration.

DENISE: That's so great, Coleen! Like Ray, Tim loved it when I was pregnant. Some men don't like the look or the feel of a woman in pregnancy, but he embraced the whole thing. There are men who don't find women sexually attractive when they are pregnant, whereas I often wished that Tim wouldn't find me sexually attractive, so I could get a break! No, but seriously, he loved both my pregnancies and was very supportive. He had to be, because there were some real mood swings going on there!

SHERRIE: My dad was very supportive during my pregnancy, because he was living with us then. He and I went everywhere together. I think my husband was glad that somebody else was there to be with me, so that he didn't have to be. At the time, he was working at British Aerospace; he'd leave the house at 7a.m. and not come back until 8p.m., so I didn't see much of him. As a result, he was never really part of the pregnancy. My father was, but it kind of passed my husband by.

Although my father lived with me, my mother was a constant support, a tower of strength. This meant that I could work, because I had a permanent babysitter. If I'd had a choice, I wouldn't have gone back to work for at least six months. But I had no choice. My parents provided me with the strength that I needed. My husband was in and out, in the same way that my dad was when I was a child, funnily enough.

How different are the roles of father and mother?

DENISE: Tim and I don't really have defined roles at all; at least, they're a lot less defined than they are for a lot of couples. The nature of our work means that sometimes Tim is busy and I have to hold the fort at home, which is when the children either starve or get take-outs. At other times, I am away, so Tim has to be mother, father and chef.

I'm very lucky that I can just go away and work knowing that Tim is at home. I don't mean that everything will get done; it won't. Men don't multitask very well, so the dead light bulbs won't have been changed and we'll be in blackout when I get back, but at least the children will be have been fed. Tim doesn't do DIY. He doesn't see things that need doing like that. It does bug me sometimes, but I'd much prefer him to be a good mum/dad to my kids when I am away.

We share the roles, but there are certain things Matthew will come and talk to me about, not because he feels he couldn't talk to his dad about it, but because I'm his mum. So if he and his girlfriend are having a problem or if he's upset about something, he comes and sits on the end of the bed and talks to me. He's a very sensitive kid. Tim would be equally as supportive and helpful to him; it's just that I'm his mum. That's just the way it works.

SHERRIE: I was mother and father to Keeley. There was never any discussion: I made the decisions; I chose the schools; I picked out the clothes; I went to sports days and parents meetings; I took her on holiday. He never came to a nativity play and I never expected him to. It never occurred to me that there was anybody else in that relationship.

Sometimes her dad was there and sometimes not. I don't want to be unfair to him, because I'm sure he loved her, but he didn't necessarily want children; it was not a world he wanted. So she was mine from the day she was born. That was the end of the story. I know it sounds strange, but it's the way our life was. I guess that's why I didn't have any more children, because he was not a child person.

How do you bring up a son to be a good man?

DENISE: It's difficult. Tim and I have never sat down with a planner and worked out what we should do. Instead, Matthew has learnt from the people he has been around and the way his dad has been with me. Fortunately, Tim loves women. He loves his male friends, but he also enjoys being around women. Some people say, 'Tim's a proper man's man.' But just because he goes to the pub and doesn't like wine bars doesn't mean he doesn't also like women's company.

I'm very proud of Matthew's attitude to women. I really do feel that we've done something right with Matthew to help him become the rounded human being that he is. He is generally without prejudice and he has total respect for women and really loves to be around them. He also loves to be around men. He opens doors and he stands up for women, neither of which are things we have pressed him into. He naturally does it. I know the feminist brigade would say that they don't want that, but he would do it for men too, because he's a genuinely respectful person.

Sometimes I've said to Matthew, 'Yes, I have made this or that mistake. Yes, you have witnessed your dad saying that to me. It doesn't mean you have to do it. That's our relationship. We're just two people who met and fell in love. But the mistakes we've made are wrong.' He seems to have taken it on board when I've said to him, 'Do as we say, not as we do!' However, I strongly believe that if he were living in an unhealthy environment witnessing an unhealthy relationship, he would not be the man he is now.

Tim and I know that we have got some things wrong in life, but we do think we have got it right with Matthew. I love seeing my friends having conversations with him; I can see how he affects them and touches them. And how intelligent he is. Afterwards, they all say to me or to each other, 'Oh my God, I just could have talked to Matthew all night!'

LYNDA: Oh God, it makes me so proud when that happens! Because it can be a challenge to bring boys up well. Depending on your relationship with their father, they might pick up lack of respect or kindness or see their mother put on a pedestal, which isn't helpful either. It can result in cruelty.

I probably denied my sons some of the rough and tumble they should have had, because of my marriage being fraught. I tried to protect them and restrain them, when I should have encouraged them to get out there and fight. I think they took it as a sign of weakness in me and they didn't respect that.

Fathers are much harder and tougher with their sons than

mums are – and that's what boys need. This is where they suffer when there aren't two parents, especially in their teens. When they are little, it doesn't matter so much. I'm sorry that my father wasn't there for my sons more when my marriage to their father ended, because I'm sure it would have helped them. The man-to-man relationship is important and very different.

Is it a disaster if a woman earns more than a man?

COLEEN: I suppose I've grown up more of a traditionalist. I quite like the fact that men do certain things and women do certain things. People might say that I'm the one out working, but if my husband was lucky enough to become the main breadwinner, I would be happy to stay at home. I think it's just that life has dealt me that hand and I'm the main bread-winner, so I have to work. I'm very lucky in what I do.

When I was married to Shane and I gave up the business to be a stay-at-home mum for two and a half years, I absolutely loved it and didn't feel guilty at all. It was probably the hardest two and a half years of my life, though! Being a housewife is a 24/7 job with no thanks and no pay. At least with the job I do now, I get people coming up to me in the street saying, 'I loved you on that show!' or 'Didn't you do well?' Or I get applause when I go out on stage. When you're a mum, you don't get any of that. Well, not until your children grow up a bit, anyway. Now that my two eldest are twenty-one and seventeen, I get more thanks, but when children are younger, you're just a pain that tells them what they can and can't do.

People say, 'You should know what's under the bonnet of your own car. You should be able to do all that DIY stuff.' I think, I don't want to! I've got a man who can do that and I like it that way!

I think that women have made men quite insecure about what their role is because we are trying to be superwomen who can do everything ourselves, who don't actually need men until we want children – and nowadays we don't need them for that, either! We just need a good turkey baster and we're away. So I feel quite sorry for men.

Having said all that, I'm still very much in favour of equal working rights and equal pay for women. And what's great is that women without men are accepted more these days; no one looks down their nose at you if you're a single parent; if your marriage doesn't work, people don't point the finger if you've left. I think that's great. I'm glad that many of the prejudices that held women back have disappeared, but I still like men to be men and I like to sometimes play the 'little woman' who needs a man. Maybe I am a feminist after all – a clever feminist!

I think it really hurts the male ego when a woman earns more than the man; it doesn't seem to be as acceptable socially, either. When I stopped working and became a stay-at-home mum while I was married to Shane, nobody ever commented. But they do make comments to Ray. There's more of a stigma. All of a sudden, it's, 'Oh, he doesn't mind that she goes out to work!' I think, you never said that to me when it was the other way round. People are still sexist when it comes to that.

Ray is so supportive and I couldn't do without him in so many ways. He sorts all the behind-the-scenes stuff out for me, because I am useless when it comes to money and business organisation. I'm also rubbish at DIY and sorting things out around the house, whereas he's brilliant at it. If something breaks, it's fixed. He's fantastic but no one sees that. It's like being a stay-at-home parent: you don't get applause for this stuff.

My husband is really proud of what I do, but as a man, I know he would love it to be the other way round. He loves what he does; he's a musician by trade, so he does work, but it's sporadic, irregular work. It makes him die, because sometimes I say, 'I want to come home! I wish I could just come home.' 'It's so weird, isn't it?' he says. 'I would love to be out there as much as you, and yet you just want to come home.'

I constantly tell him how much I need him, because I do. I would collapse without him; I wouldn't know what to do. It's a partnership and you have to make your partner feel needed. So as long as I continue to make him feel needed, it will be all right, although it must be hard for him at times. Praise is important. It's worth doing, even if you're saying it through gritted teeth.

DENISE: There can be lots of problems when the woman in the relationship becomes the major breadwinner. It's not necessarily hard for the woman as such, but it can be hard for the woman because it's hard for the man.

It's social conditioning that we expect the man to be the major breadwinner and even a very modern man wants it to be that way. In my experience, most relationships work better if that is the case. I have seen it work the other way round, though. For instance, because Tim and I are actors, there have been times when Tim has been the major breadwinner and provider and there have been other times when I've had that role. But, to be honest, he would still prefer it to be the conventional way round.

I notice a shift in our relationship when Tim is in the bread-winner role. He might deny it, but he seems much happier and confident when he is out working and providing and I am at home. Of course, I won't be at home *cooking*, because of my particular inability to do that particular chore, but he loves it if I'm at home nurturing. If he's going away and I'm not work-ing, I will pack his case for him and he loves that. Obviously, if I'm working, I don't have the time to do it.

He operates better if our roles are predictably Mummy, Daddy and children. It's partly because society tends to define those positions, but it also mirrors his background. Although his mum worked, he was from a family where Dad worked hard and therefore Dad got the cut of meat at the weekend if there was only one cut to be had – and Mum and the children went without.

SHERRIE: I think it's harder for men now that women are so much stronger. It's confusing for them. I have always been the breadwinner and had the earning power, which can be very difficult for a man. His power as the hunter is gone and the woman becomes the hunter. Who has the power in the family then?

ANDREA: Does somebody have to have the power?

SHERRIE: Yes, because you can't be equal, although that's what we've striven for all our lives. I don't think equality is possible, because we are not the same.

My mother always earned her own money. She always worked hard and was always the breadwinner. In the same way, I had to work, because I was the money earner; I had no other choice. I didn't have the option of saying, 'I'm having a baby and so I'm not going to work for a year.' I had to go back to work within weeks of having Keeley. My father was living with me then. He came to live with me when Keeley was born and became her nanny, which was the only way I could work. My mother was also always there for me. I knew I could always turn to her and rely on her.

Having no choices toughened me up and that saddens me. I didn't have the kind of relationship in which I could say, 'I don't have to do this job; I'm going to sit back now.' Whatever came in, I had to take. One of my biggest regrets is that I took jobs that I shouldn't have taken, because that was where the money was. My career was going one way and then it turned. After doing a wonderful television film called *Kate the Good Neighbour* with Rachel Kempson in 1980, I was up for a BAFTA and planned to go to America to make a film. Unfortunately, a job came in here offering a lot of money and my agent said, 'Take it, because it's going to earn you mega money.'

I asked my husband what he thought and he said, 'We need that money. We have to pay the mortgage.' 'OK,' I said. I always wonder what would have happened if I had gone the way I wanted to. I really wanted to go to America and make films, but I gave up the chance for money. You should never give anything up for money and you should never work purely for money, because it will always come and bite you on the bum. Just take a chance.

At the time, I felt I had to earn as much as possible, because I had to pay the bills and the mortgage; I had a baby and a husband and my father at home. If it meant going a certain route, which was probably not the route I would have chosen, well that's what I had to do.

Had it been another time with somebody else, I would have given up work for a year. Maybe I would have had another baby, too. But I didn't have the choice, and without choices you are buggered. Still, regrets are futile. You can't regret anything.

DENISE: Did being the breadwinner have a major effect on your relationship, then?

SHERRIE: Yes, because I had to be tough. I couldn't allow one little chink; there was no room for weakness. I was constantly having to plan ahead and take more work to pay my tax. I was living in a time when we were paying 17 per cent interest on our mortgages. Can you believe that? Whatever you earned was gone within days. There was no way you could save or have a pension plan. It was terrible; you had to have money coming in all the time, or you lost everything. In that situation, you lose your sense of life. I had to become the man, even though I didn't want to be a man; I wanted to be a wife and a mother.

Don't get me wrong: I wouldn't have been happy without a career. I have always been career oriented and I love my job. I'm a creative person, so I would have either acted or written, but I wanted the option of staying at home and of saying no to that job because I didn't feel it was the right job for me. It was wrong for me to go the way I did.

LYNDA: It's sad that you feel that way, Sherrie. I know exactly what you mean. If the two of you have to work to live at a certain standard when you first get together, that's terrific. But if children are involved, there is inevitably going to come a point where somebody is going to have to compromise their career to look after the kids. Nine times out of ten it is going to be the woman, just naturally. OK, it's not fair. Why should a man be able to go off and have his career while you stay at home? Well, that's how it works most of the time. You can analyse it until the cows come home, but that's the way it is. If your man becomes a househusband as a matter of course, that is fine too. In the main, I would suggest that the decision is made naturally.

Sometimes it's hard to say this to a woman, but it is so rewarding when you have children and you run a home brilliantly, when your husband glows and flourishes and you send him off confident. It is a fantastic feeling of nurture. If he subsequently goes off and has an affair with his secretary, it won't be because you are at home. It will be because he has a problem, or there is a problem in the marriage.

When it comes to my husband and sons, I clearly see their need for a base and to be cherished and nurtured. I love doing this for them. It makes me feel completely fulfilled. Yes, of course women want to be cherished and nurtured too, but it is much more in our natures to do it than it is for men. Women complain and say, 'My husband never sends me flowers.' I always say, 'You will get it in other ways.'

Fortunately for me, though, I've never been asked to give up my career.

DENISE: Does it really have to be one or the other?

LYNDA: I think that you can be dependent on a man financially and still have an individual life, even without having a career. There is lots to do out there, from volunteer work to history of art courses. If you have to work part time, that's life. People have to get over themselves. My sister works in an opticians. OK, it is not the height of intellectual prowess, but it fits in with her life.

I'm brilliant at cleaning and I would love to see the day when it would be acceptable for me to go off and clean. Maybe it's the actress in me, but when we were doing up our villa in Spain, which he bought, I said to Mr Spain, 'We could do it up in a way that meant that if I can't get any work, I could run this as a B&B.' He laughed. 'Why not?' I asked. 'Why wouldn't I? If I couldn't work and I had to earn a living doing something else, that's what I'd be happy doing.' Don't get me wrong: that wouldn't be the case if I were about to embark on an amazing career in Hollywood, but life is about adapting and recognising what makes you happy.

Sometimes men and women are so concentrated on the outside influences that they forget to look at what is good about men and women together in a relationship.

SHERRIE: Wise words, Lynda! How about you, Lisa? What do you think about this?

LISA: I don't expect Paul to provide for the family but he is quite old fashioned in that way and wants to do it. I think it can be a disaster if the woman earns more, if it goes on for a long period of time. It can emasculate the man if he thinks he's not doing what a man is supposed to do. But if you've got a sound enough relationship and you're clear enough about your own roles, as a couple, then within that framework, everybody should be fine. You probably need to set out your stall quite early on.

I've always earned money and I've always enjoyed having the freedom and independence of having my own money. I don't like to be beholden to somebody for finances, it makes me uncomfortable. But I don't have an issue with supporting a man, and never have. The thing is that most of the men I've been with, did have an issue with it.

As it turns out, I've only ever had serious relationships with actors or self-employed people. Paul is self-employed and I'm self-employed and we're very much of a mind that whoever is earning at the time puts money in the pot. I'm not counting, either. I might put in £2.50 and he puts in £2, or vice versa. Also, when you have kids, it doesn't matter where it comes from. It's for the good of the family. So, whatever you've got, put it in the pot!

Paul is incredibly generous and I can have anything I want. He absolutely enjoys spoiling me: nice holidays and clothes etc. He likes to see me looking nice, not in a controlling way, but he gets excited when he thinks he's found a jumper that I'll love. If he's in town, he'll buy it for me, and I love that about him.

Have you ever issued your man with an ultimatum and do they ever really work?

DENISE: I have issued them and I do issue them to Tim, but they rarely work. Recently, I got fed up with him not doing certain little jobs around the house, so I put a ban on sex, but he hasn't noticed! I don't think he even cares! So the door handles are still falling off. I'm always doing it with the kids, but that's more of a discipline thing. I don't respond well to ultimatums if Tim tries to issue them; I just dig my heels in even more.

KATE: They're something we all associate with our childhoods, because it's how we were parented and it's how we parent.

COLEEN: And then you get into your forties and think, don't talk to me like I'm a child! I can't bear ultimatums, because if you issue one and they do what you've asked them to, you think, well, they haven't done it because they wanted to or because they were being kind, they've done it because you said, 'If you don't . . .'

SHERRIE: So it's a bit like nagging, isn't it?

COLEEN: Yes, it makes me feel like a nag.

KATE: I agree; it devalues the end result, because it's begrudged.

COLEEN: Yes, and if somebody says to me, 'If you don't stop doing that, I'm not going to speak to you,' then I will do it more! Don't tell me what to do now that I'm an adult! It wouldn't work, anyway. If I gave Ray ultimatums, he'd just say, 'See you, then!'

DENISE: I'm such a hypocrite as well, because I drink, but when Tim gets drunk, I say, 'You're absolutely disgusting, the amount you drink. I won't be here for much longer if you come home in that state anymore!'

SHERRIE: *You* say that? That'll make him drink more!

DENISE: Well, it does! And it makes me drink more!

KATE: Den, you are the pot calling the kettle black!

DENISE: I know, but at least I've admitted that I'm a hypocrite.

KATE: Darren has never given me an ultimatum and I've never issued him with one, because he would just tell me where to go, frankly. But he did say to me, 'You'll never, ever be able to give up smoking!' and I did it because I wanted to prove him wrong. But he should have been very careful what he wished for, because I gave up and then we went on holiday together and he had to spend all that time on his own with me and I was a bit of a mess. I'd be in tears every night when it got to cigarette time. In the end, he had to lie to the people in the hotel we were staying in: he said our dog had died! We didn't even have a dog!

SHERRIE: My ex could drink for England, but in a fun way, because he never got hangovers. He used to say to me when we went out, 'Are you sure you want another glass of wine?' It made me so mad. I'd say, 'Oh really?' Then I'd drink and drink. Unfortunately, I'd be ill for days afterwards and he'd say, 'I rest my case . . .' He was right, but I had to do it because I couldn't bear the fact that he was right and I was wrong!

KATE: That's the problem with being told what to do, isn't it?

COLEEN: If you've been trying to lose weight, as I have over the last few years, the worst thing for a woman is to be reminded of her diet. Last Christmas I thought, no, it's Christmas, I'm going to do what I want and stop obsessing about food, then I'll start watching what I eat again in the new year. In the meantime, I'm going to eat like a horse. Which I did! A Shire horse! Of course, by Boxing Day, Ray's saying, 'Diet's going well, then . . .'

KATE: No! Did you kick him?

COLEEN: It's not a good thing for a man to say to a woman . . . but his funeral was lovely the week later! I sent lovely flowers and a bar of chocolate.

DENISE: I wouldn't normally speak up on behalf of Ray on this show, but to give him his due, it's not because he wants you to lose weight, it's because he knows how miserable you are when you put it on.

COLEEN: It's true; he knows that by January, I'll be moaning, 'I wish I hadn't eaten so much at Christmas, because now I've got to get rid of the weight.'

SHERRIE: See – you knew he was right – and that's what makes ultimatums wrong.

COLEEN: Shhhh! I haven't told him he was right!

Should you express your gratitude and appreciation to your partner five times a day, as Oprah Winfrey recommends?

LISA: You have to have your five a day of everything now, don't you? I try to say thank you to Paul when he does something nice, which is a lot of the time. But I think it would be really annoying to keep saying thank you. 'Thank you for being you.' 'Thank you for your nice colour hair.' 'Thank you for being the father of my child.' Five times a day is a lot, I think!

JANE: If they *genuinely* help you, then it's nice to say thank you. I've had different partners along the way and I actually have a partner now who is very helpful. I am so grateful, because he does empty the dishwasher, he does make the bed and he does put the towels back where I want them. So I say, 'Wow, thanks a lot!'

SHERRIE: You don't have to thank him for making the bed, Jane.

JANE: I think it is nice to acknowledge that someone has done something nice for you.

SHERRIE: Why can't he just make the bed? Why do you have to say thank you?

JANE: I just think it's nice when you help each other. He will say, 'Thanks for sorting my suit out. Thanks for . . .'

LISA: . . . five times a day?

JANE: Oh, more. More, more!

LISA: What five things does he do for you in any one day?

JANE: Well, it's been that long he's been away now that I can't remember, to be quite honest!

ANDREA: I'm sure you'll be able to thank him more than five times a day when he gets back!

JANE: I think I will.

ANDREA: I must admit, Steve is pretty good and I do try and say thank you. But I'm a bit rubbish, a bit distracted and I suppose I do take a little bit for granted. So I think I should maybe try harder. That would be my school report.

LISA: Note to self. Be nicer.

ANDREA: Note to self. Must try harder. Yes, generally be nicer.

SHERRIE: I have to say that Ken never did anything, so I had nothing to thank him for.

ANDREA: The lovely Keeley!

SHERRIE: My Keeley, yes.

LISA: A hundred times a day!

Do you like to praise your man in public?

KATE: When Catherine Zeta Jones won the Tony award for her role in the Broadway musical *A Little Night Music*, in her excitement, she gave a rather gushing speech that included an intimate tribute to her 66-year-old husband Michael Douglas. She said, 'See that man there? He's a movie star and I get to sleep with him every night!' Clearly, she thinks her man is great and she wanted to tell the world how marvellous he is. Do you ever get the urge to shower your man with praise and tell anyone who will listen?

CAROL: Well, no, not unsolicited! I don't walk around the streets with a banner and I don't shout out all the time how fantastic he is, unless somebody asks me. If somebody asks me, 'What's Mark like?' I will tell them, 'He's amazing! I love him.' Why not? He is gorgeous. He's perfect . . . I could go on, but I won't, because I haven't won an award. If I'd won an award, I might well do what she did.

KATE: I have to say you always speak so beautifully of Mark and with such respect. That's so lovely to hear, because you are a lone voice.

CAROL: Only if I'm asked. That is the important thing. I don't think there's anything wrong with showering praise on somebody who you adore, if people are interested. But I don't go and tell everybody.

KATE: Do you tell him?

CAROL: Of course! All the time.

KATE: You do that with Ray don't you, Coleen?

COLEEN: All the time.

KATE: That ego has been so well massaged by the hand of the Nolan.

COLEEN: Honestly, he thinks he's a god, that man! That's because I keep saying, 'Oh God!' every time I come home. No, but it's all about having a happy balance. When he is being marvellous and wonderful and I do adore him, then I love telling people. But when he is being the complete opposite of all of those things, I *adore* telling people!

You know when you're with your girlfriends and you're complaining, 'He did this last night. It really got on my nerves!'. Your friends will usually say, 'Yes, mine does that!' Well, we had this one friend who always said, 'Mine never does that.' Their marriage was so perfect. So there was a really nasty part of me that had to laugh when they got divorced!

KATE: I had a friend like that and actually I think that it masked a lot of problems at home. We used to call her Bree Van De Kamp, after the character in *Desperate Housewives* who always has a meringue in her hand and thinks everything is fabulous.

COLEEN: Maybe for some people it is genuinely like that. They just adore them 24 hours a day, seven days a week.

KATE: There is a huge difference in age between my friend Nicky and her husband. He was 18 when they met and she was in her 30s. We all wrote it off and said, 'This will never last.' But it so has and they are still happily married. Every time I say to her, 'And how's Charlie?' she says, 'Mmm, he's lovely!' and she means it. They are so deliciously happy together and it's magnetic.

CAROL: See? Not everyone's bitter!

COLEEN: He must get on her nerves sometimes.

KATE: No! OK, there are little niggles sometimes . . .

COLEEN: Niggles! That's what I mean.

CAROL: But you don't have to tell everybody. I've never really listened too much to girlfriends who go on and on about how awful their partners are, because I think, if they're that awful, then do something about it and stop boring everybody with it. Women do go on and on about it, all the time.

COLEEN: I know, but then you discuss it with your friends and say, 'He's really getting on my nerves.' But if your friends say, 'Yes, I don't like that about him, either,' you say, 'What do you mean, you don't like him?' I'm allowed not to like him but you have to like him!

Do you think it's important that our men boost our confidence?

CAROL: It depends how much you need it. For instance, I'm not quite as confident as everybody thinks I am. It's a bit of a misconception, because I'm quite shy sometimes and not very confident about my own abilities. Mark's very good like that: he does tell me that I'm really good at certain things.

LISA: Ooh!

CAROL: No, I'm talking about my work, usually: I never think that anything I write is any good. But he's very good. He never says anything bad about me.

The worst thing is that, because he's younger, you're going to have a crisis of confidence every now and again. I mean, I'm fifty now and you do sometimes look in the mirror and think, oh no! So I occasionally say certain things and he just banishes them, as if he hasn't noticed. He's very good like that and, although I believe him when he says it, I still don't quite believe *it*.

ANDREA: Do you need it from him?

CAROL: I wouldn't say I need it, because I'm quite good at boosting my own confidence, in a way. I think about it quite a lot. I try not to put myself down all the time. I think that's one of the secrets of confidence.

LISA: As long as he thinks you're great, that's all that matters.

CAROL: I think it is, yes, but you have to think you're great as well, yourself.

LISA: You have to believe it and if it's someone you trust and they don't generally pander to you, if they're straight talkers, then it's great when they give you a compliment. Paul's a bit like that: he's very straight and he's been so supportive, especially recently, with my nan dying. He made me believe that I could actually take on a lot more than I thought I could. I think I would have crumbled, had he not been so great.

ANDREA: More than you could take on, emotionally, do you mean?

LISA: Yes, for instance, I arranged the funeral and I've never arranged a funeral before. I didn't think that I would be grown up enough to be able to cope with it, but he wouldn't have any of it. He convinced me that I could do it.

Equally, Paul has always wanted a family and I kind of pretended that I did in the first couple of years when we were together, but I didn't really, because I was scared of it. He convinced me that I wouldn't be a rubbish mum. He said, 'I think you'd be great.' For years, I would never have considered having a child, but he made me believe that I could do the job. Thank God he did, because we now have a lovely girl. So I think it can be amazing if your partner gives you confidence.

ANDREA: As Carol says, you need to have an in-built belief in yourself, even if you're not always that confident in what you're doing, but it's also nice to have someone back you up.

One thing that Steve does is that, when I'm leaving to go somewhere, I ask him, 'What do you think I should wear?' Although he's a big, burly builder, he actually has quite a good eye for what looks nice and what doesn't look nice, and he is brutally honest. He'll say, 'No, that doesn't look nice, but that looks great!' Because he's honest, I believe him. If he just said that everything looked lovely, I wouldn't believe him. As I go to the door, he'll say, 'Knock 'em bandy!' It's lovely! You go out feeling confident.

CAROL: Normally, if you ask a bloke, 'Does this look nice?' they'll scan your eyes, thinking, what's the answer? Can I phone a friend? I don't know!

SHERRIE: Being Billy No-Mates, I can't talk about my partner.

LISA: We're your mates!

SHERRIE: Thank you, that's the correct answer. Anyway, I look to my women friends if I need a boost in confidence – and as you well know, I do need a boost in confidence. When you've been through certain things, you sometimes find it hard to come back. I feel OK now, but in a way I wish that ten years ago I'd had the confidence that's coming back now. I often think, why didn't it come back then?

ANDREA: Everybody feels that to a certain extent. As you get older, you think, if I'd had this head on that body, it would have been a really good mix.

CAROL: Do you believe people though, Sherrie? Everyone's always trying to tell you how great you look, but I don't know if you believe it. Sometimes I think you do, but . . .

SHERRIE: It's really hard, though. You say, 'Thanks!' I know why you're saying it, but thanks very much all the same.

Do you ever find comfort in someone else's relationship misery?

DENISE: Not per se, no. The only time that I find pleasure in it is when it's couples who gloat about their happiness and criticise other people's relationships. I think that each relationship is special to the couple in it, and it doesn't matter how you get through. There have been a couple of break-ups in the press lately that made me go, 'Nah, nah-na-na-nah!' because they have gloated about their 'perfect' life on many occasions and criticised others. So I do get off on their misery!

SHERRIE: I had a friend who was going through a very bad time in her relationship and I went round to hers and sat with her and listened and took on everything she said. I left her, thinking, isn't it great that I haven't got these problems! It made me feel slightly better, I suppose. Then I got home and started to think, actually, I think I *have* got those problems! Then I started to look at myself and my relationship. It opened my eyes.

ANDREA: But how about the fact that you're single now? How

does it make you feel when you listen to other friends who have relationship problems? Is there a little part of you that's kind of glad?

SHERRIE: That they're breaking up? No, that would be horrible to say that, Andrea! I wouldn't say that. Lots of women of my age are on their own now and you have to learn to live with it. You cannot look at a relationship and think in that way, because you'd come over as bitter and sad and twisted.

LISA: I think misery likes company.

SHERRIE: Do you? I'm not sure what that means!

LISA: I mean that if someone's got the hump, they're not happy unless you've got the hump as well.

ANDREA: That was very nicely put!

LISA: Obviously, when kids are involved, that puts a totally different slant on it and I always think that it's really sad when a couple who have kids break-up. I don't take any comfort in that, at all. It's absolutely heartbreaking.

But often people come and talk to Paul and me, because we're quite open, honest people. They'll share their problems with us and later Paul and I will have a chat about what they should do about them. We sit there and talk as if it's all perfect with us and say, 'Well, perhaps if she was a bit more like this and he was a little less like that . . .' Then we look at each other and say, 'You're a bit like that, aren't you?'

SHERRIE: That's what I mean! You do it to yourself! But sometimes, when I listen to other people, I think, actually, I wasn't such a failure. Maybe things do go wrong. If that's happened to them and they can come out of it, maybe it's OK for it to go wrong. Because you feel a failure when your marriage breaks up.

ANDREA: Actually, being a failure can be quite a positive thing. I know when I was trying to be Mrs Stepford Wife the whole time, wafting around saying, 'Everything's all lovely! Look what I've baked!' just like Bree in *Desperate Housewives* . . .

LISA: If you don't mind me saying, he's better off without you, if you were like that!

ANDREA: He is! I thought that you had to make everything appear absolutely lovely to the outside world, because you didn't talk about things. You brushed them under the carpet. Then everything exploded spectacularly, it all fell apart, the dust settled and we went on to be very happy in different relationships, but for a while I felt like a massive failure. Not only to myself and family; I also thought that other people would look at me that way. Now I think completely the opposite. I think, no, I'm just a normal person. It's not a bad thing to fail.

LISA: Now you can give advice to friends.

ANDREA: I wouldn't necessarily give advice, but I would listen and be far more empathetic.

DENISE: I can understand that people feel very envious when they look at Tim and me and see the perfect relationship. It makes them feel a little bit insecure and I can't help that.

SHERRIE: I was going to say the same! I think, wow, look at those two!

DENISE: Yes, well that's life!

LISA: You do get on fantastically well. You make each other laugh.

DENISE: I have to say, we've been together for 21 years and it's great!

It's funny, this thing about taking pleasure in other people's relationship pain. When I was eleven I had a friend who used to love to say to me, 'I'd hate to live in your house, because your mum and dad are always rowing.' OK, she did witness the fight between them when my mum was brandishing a toasting fork and my dad a knotted tea towel, but she used to say, 'It must be awful! My mum and dad never argue.' Well, guess who's divorced? Not my parents! So I think you shouldn't comment on other people's relationships, unless you're asked to.

ANDREA: Exactly!

Do you keep quiet about the things your partner tells you? Do you want them to keep quiet about the things you tell them?

CAROL: I'm quite trustworthy, believe it or not. If someone tells me not to tell anyone, I don't tell anyone. One of my friends was pregnant and she didn't want anybody to know. I didn't even tell Mark and I was quite pleased with myself.

LYNDA: That's very good.

CAROL: Mark can know anything he wants, but I'm not about to sit there and go through it all. I mean, I've written it all in a book, so he can read that and then he will know everything. While I was writing it, I think he thought I was trying to keep it from him. One day I went home and he said, 'Did you have sex in a sauna?' 'Yes, why? How do you know that?' I asked. It turned out that a page from the book that I had printed was in the shredder and he read it while he was doing the shredding!

LYNDA: When I was writing my book, Mr Spain read each chapter as I wrote it. He kept saying, 'Not another bloke! Can't we lose a few of these?' Excuse me!

I am very lucky, actually, and he knows most things. I would never think, I'd better go through the whole list of exes before we get any further.

On the other hand, if I had a girlfriend who told me something that I thought might colour his opinion of her, I probably wouldn't tell. They can be funny, blokes, sometimes.

LISA: If a girlfriend confides in me and she knows Paul as well, I will say, 'Is it a secret, or can I tell Paul?' If she didn't mind, then I'd probably tell him. But I don't think blokes want to know everything and there are things in my past that I'm quite pleased Paul doesn't know about. I was a fully formed person with a past before I met him and every now and then I have a think about it and it makes me smile.

I think I know about his past, but I think he has probably been quite careful about what he has given away, as well. There is a massive responsibility involved in telling somebody a secret, because in some ways you're dumping it on them, if you know what I mean. You have to take responsibility.

Is it important for your sleep patterns to be compatible?

COLEEN: Ray, bless him, snores like a pig. He'll swear blind that he doesn't, but he does. He sleeps on his back with his arms folded, and he cocoons himself in the duvet so I can't get near him. What's that all about? So I start by nudging him a bit, because if I nudge him, he'll turn on his side and stop snoring. But five seconds later he turns back and starts snoring again. By about four o'clock in the morning, I'm kicking him, pinching him and yelling, 'Shut up!'

He's a nightmare. However, so am I, apparently, because I cry in my sleep every night. I don't know why; it's probably over his snoring, to be honest! I cry and shout out in my sleep and it drives him nuts.

KATE: That's an interesting insight into your state of mind, Col.

COLEEN: I know, I've obviously been doing this job too long.

KATE: I always roll into Darren's part of the bed, because he's bigger than me. I think most men are bigger than their female partners, aren't they? One would hope so, anyway. Poor Katie Holmes!

Darren's a snorer too. The other night he was making such weird noises that I thought a bird had got into our son Ben's nursery and I could hear it on the monitor. So I was up there, in the middle of the night, like Angela Lansbury, thinking, where's that noise coming from? Then I came downstairs and realised that Darren's got a bit of a cold and it was one of his nostrils!

JANE: My bed is that big, there's a bus stop in the middle of it! I just like big beds; I don't know why, because there's wasn't anyone else in it for such a long time. But my Ed is actually the perfect sleeping partner. He goes to sleep with a smile on his face – of course, when I'm there! He doesn't snore and then wakes up with the same smile in the same exact position. So that's lovely. He's a real good spooner, too.

COLEEN: Spooning? Oh no.

JANE: I love spooning; it keeps me warm. I switch the heat down in the bedroom, you see, because by God it gets hot after a while . . . Ha! I'm such a liar!

COLEEN: Spooning, no. I like a little cuddle when I get into bed, for about five seconds, and then my back's turned on him and it's like, stay away! He's the same.

KATE: That sounds like the secret of a successful marriage!

Would you mind your man wearing a pair of striped pyjamas in bed?

LISA: Yes, I would! It's like putting a suit on to go to bed! It's a bit odd, don't you think?

DENISE: Don't you wear them?

LISA: I'm naked in bed.

DENISE: Are you?

LISA: So is Paul! Why would you put all that stuff on to go to bed?

SHERRIE: I think a man with sexy bottoms on is quite nice, don't you, girls? If they're quite low-slung bottoms . . .

LISA: It's not hygienic!

SHERRIE: What's not hygienic?

DENISE: I know what you mean, Sherrie. I think boxers can be

OK, but I don't think it would be very nice if you'd just slept with someone and they popped off to put on a pair of stripy 'jamas.

We had Louis's little friend to stay over the other night and his mum sent me this text about her son: 'He made me laugh so much when he told me about being in Tim's room, playing football. He said, "Do you know that Denise sleeps in a different room to Tim, because he sleeps naked and snores a bit?"'

SHERRIE: That's so sweet!

ANDREA: How old is he?

DENISE: He's nine. The thing is, Tim does sleep naked, but it's me that snores a bit! I don't really like sleeping naked, because I think certain areas should be saved, to be seen only at certain times.

SHERRIE: I agree!

DENISE: I think that it's just not attractive to see those areas when one of you is going for a wee in the middle of the night.

LISA: But if you can't get the bits out in bed, when can you?

SHERRIE: But they're all in bed then, aren't they? It's better when they're put away, isn't it?

LISA: No, you should only put on all that stuff if you're going into hospital!

ANDREA: I think pyjamas can be quite cute.

DENISE: What does Steve wear in bed, tell me, Andrea? (Pant! pant!)

ANDREA: Obviously, he's a builder, so he comes home from work quite dirty.

DENISE: Ooh!

ANDREA: Not in that way! I mean, muddy! So he'll go and have a shower and, if it's fairly late, he'll put on what you might call his loungey pyjamas. He takes those off to go to bed, so he actually doesn't wear anything in bed, because he gets really hot.

DENISE: (Whimper!)

SHERRIE: He's enormous, your Steve, isn't he?

ANDREA: He is, he's very tall! Oh, he fills a pyjama, does my Steve!

DENISE: And they all keep their bananas in their pyjamas!

When you're in a relationship, how important is it to go on flirting?

LISA: I don't really know how to flirt with Paul now. We flirted a lot when we got together, but we've been through so much since then that it would seem a bit trivial if I

started flirting with him. After going through something
life changing like having a child, I don't think I need to
start giving him the eye! He would think there was something wrong!

And, you know, I feel a bit uncomfortable if I'm just about
to get in the bath and I run down the hallway naked to get
something and he says, 'Phwoar!'

DENISE: If I ran through the house naked, Tim would say,
'That needs an iron!' I can't bear it when they see you naked.
It makes me hurry up to put some clothes on, because I think,
oh please don't want jiggy-jigs when I want to watch some
telly!

ANDREA: Do you flirt, you two?

DENISE: I think if I started flirting with him across the table,
he'd say, 'Have you got something in your eye?' In fact,
when we were at Carol's fiftieth birthday party in Bangkok,
on the night of her party, he was really sober and he got up
and sang and everyone was saying, 'Isn't he wonderful?' For
the first time in quite a long time, I thought, I really quite
fancy my husband tonight! So I gave him a kiss, a proper
kiss, and he wiped his mouth in disgust and said, 'What
did you do that for?' So I couldn't even flirt with him if I
tried!

LISA: I think you get beyond it.

SHERRIE: I think flirting is quite nice. When I was with my
ex, in happier times, we did flirt. For instance, when I went

to stay with a friend, I'd say, 'Meet me tomorrow in London and we'll go for dinner.' It was like having a date. You have to like somebody a lot to do that, because you have to work really hard at it and it takes a long time to set it up. So you have to care about somebody to flirt.

LISA: I think you need to not know them!

SHERRIE: No, you just have to bring a bit of romance, a bit of fantasy and a bit of Disneyland back into your life.

DENISE: Please, not that pretending-you-don't-know-each-other-at-a-bar thing! I'd just get the giggles, wouldn't you?

LISA: Although, I have to say that if I see Paul in the street, or if we've arranged to meet at a train station, and he's not aware that I'm watching him, so I'm seeing him in his own world, I find that quite sexy.

SHERRIE: Do you?

LISA: Yes, I think, that's my man over there! And I'm able to see him objectively.

DENISE: But if that were Tim, he'd be picking his nose or something!

ANDREA: And if someone doesn't know that they're being watched, they can look a little bit gormless.

LISA: No, it's when you look at them, expecting them to be

gormless, and they're not. You think, Mmm, that's my man over there. He's lovely.

ANDREA: I've been a bit poorly for the last couple of weeks and this morning was the first time for ages that I woke up and felt like me, as opposed to some creature from the Black Lagoon, which I have been feeling like and possibly acting like. I was in the shower and I thought, Steve's been a bit grumpy; ah, I know why, it's because I haven't given him enough attention. So after my shower, I got dressed; he was still in bed and I ran into the bedroom and jumped on him and yelled, 'Hi! I'm back! I feel well!'

DENISE: That's a bit too much information, Andrea MacLean!

LISA: That's not flirting; that's at least fourth base!

DENISE: That's what I call doing jiggy-jigs!

ANDREA: No, there was none of that; he had morning breath. But it made me think, maybe I will send him a little text later, just to say, 'Can't wait to see you later!' Just to keep it all a bit sparky.

SHERRIE: But do you like watching other people flirt?

DENISE: Not if they're snogging . . .

SHERRIE: When someone's in love and it's all new and they really love each other, isn't it lovely to see them?

DENISE: No, it's like being with Carol and Mark!

Can women pick out who the men in their life will find attractive?

LYNDA: No, and that's the nature of the beast. That's why attraction is so wonderful and exciting and you can never know for sure. It's nature and it's unpredictable. Thank God that no one can tamper with that magic thing, that ingredient that brings two people together.

We have become so obsessed with the superficial reasons why people find each other attractive that we have forgotten all about the mind, the intellect, the jokes and the shared experiences. But if you want something to last, that's what you have got to concentrate on.

COLEEN: Actually, I'm good at picking out women that Ray would find attractive. I think he's pretty predictable and likes your typical gorgeous young big-breasted blonde woman. Having said that, he usually says, 'OK, she's someone I might go to bed with, but I wouldn't want a relationship with her.'

I think Cheryl Cole is absolutely beautiful and a lovely girl, but Ray only thinks she's all right. He prefers Kimberley from Girls Aloud; he thinks she's stunning. Although I agree, it surprises me that he doesn't get the Cheryl Cole thing. He'd go for Danii Minogue any time; he doesn't think Cheryl's a patch on Danii. 'But the whole world thinks Cheryl Cole is beautiful!' I'll protest. 'You've got to be the only person who doesn't.'

But you know what? If Cheryl came up to him and said, 'Hi, Ray,' in her lovely Geordie accent, 'would you like to go for a drink?' I'm sure he'd go! Certainly, he wouldn't say, 'Sorry, love, I fancy Danii!' I think he'd be gone in a flash.

DENISE: Unfortunately, my son Louis finds very typical Pamela Anderson types attractive, the obvious female stereotypes that my dad always found attractive.

My boys fancy completely different types of women, though. While Louis goes for the obvious, Matthew goes for the quirky but beautiful type. So Louis would go for Pamela Anderson and Matthew would go for Agyness Deyn. I'm not sure if he actually likes Agyness Deyn, but it illustrates the difference between them. I could certainly pick out who Louis or my dad would fancy.

Sometimes women have very different ideas of what's attractive from men. Take Victoria Beckham: we think she can look fabulous and incredible stylish, but by her own admission she says that it's women who like her; men don't fancy her. I think that's probably the case with Sarah Jessica Parker as well.

LYNDA: The people you think are sexy often aren't, but there is definitely a male instinct to embrace a woman who is curvy.

DENISE: Which is good news for a lot of women, thankfully!

How do you persuade a man to do something?

COLEEN: If it was something very important to me and I definitely wanted Ray to do it, then I would say, 'I know you don't want to do it, but please do it for me.' I know he would do it then, unless it was something he totally didn't agree with.

The other thing I often try and do is turn it round so they think it's their idea in the first place. I'll pave the way so that Ray says, 'Well, why don't we do such-and-such?' I say, 'What a great idea! Brilliant! I knew I could rely on you.' Then I walk away thinking, yes!

DENISE: The nagging thing tends not to work, even though I do it, because it's always the same things that you have to remind them about. The way for me to get things done would be by being disappointed or being tearful. I have to turn on the waterworks a little bit and say how stressed I am that nobody is helping me and I just feel disappointed with them as a family that they're not giving me the support that I need. That usually achieves more than screaming, shouting and nagging, which do absolutely sweet bugger all.

Can your man still surprise you after you've been with him for years and years?

DENISE: Does Ray continue to surprise you, Coleen?

COLEEN: All the time! I find his take on things fascinating, because it can be so different to mine, especially when it comes to sex, romance and love. It can be equally as strong and passionate, but in a completely different way, so I'm endlessly curious about how he ticks.

It doesn't matter how long I am with Ray, I don't think I'll ever completely fathom him – and that's why the attraction is so strong. They say opposites attract: in some ways we're so similar and in other ways so different. It's always a blooming challenge and I don't think I'm ever going to have an easy life, because I can't work him out at all!

LISA: I've been with Paul for 14 years and he definitely still has the capacity to surprise me. He surprised me yesterday as I walked from the car to the front door carrying an Indian takeaway.

'I'm really loving you a lot today,' he said.

'What do you mean?' I said, trying to defuse his words. 'Don't be silly! Get out of the way.'

'No, I'm really loving you a lot today. I'm really lucky I've got you. You're really pretty and you've got a great personality and everybody likes you.'

He volunteered that, just because he felt it! When I tell people that, they say, 'Eurgh! It makes me feel sick!'

COLEEN: Really? Who'd have thought it?

LISA: The old me would have reacted by saying, 'What are you talking about, Paul? Don't be ridiculous! Pull yourself together. Don't be so soppy.' But we've had our ups and downs and we've had some pretty serious arguments in our time. We've come close to splitting up on a couple of occasions. So when he does say things like that, I've learned to appreciate and accept it at the time, for what it means. Instead of sweeping it away and disregarding it, if he's big enough to say it, then I have to be big enough to absorb it in the way it's meant. I think that's important.

COLEEN: Yes, but why did it surprise you if he's said things like that before?

LISA: Well, partly because I looked a fright yesterday! I think it was because he wasn't feeling very well and I made him feel looked after, which is something I'm not usually very good at.

COLEEN: So you surprised him, in fact!

LISA: Well, maybe it was a bit of both!

COLEEN: And you, Denise, can Tim still catch you unawares?

DENISE: He'll certainly give it a good try, I'll say that for him! But seriously, I don't think I totally know Tim, not at all.

LYNDA: I don't think it is possible for any human being to know another completely.

DENISE: Of course it isn't. Different things happen within the course of such a long relationship and my husband's reaction can still surprise me, sometimes for the good and sometimes not.

As an actor, I often think I know all the performances he has in him. Then occasionally I will go and see him in a play and fall in love with him all over again, because I see this different performance that I didn't know he had in him. That's quite exciting.

He is the first to admit that he is not a six-foot-three Adonis, but when he is singing or performing and I watch other women looking at him, seeing him through their eyes can also be quite exciting. I'm not someone who is always watching people's reaction to him when we go out, nor is he with me, or at least he doesn't admit it, but occasionally I'll catch an interesting glimpse of him from someone else's point of view. He sang to me on *Loose Women* on Valentine's Day and I saw lots of comments online afterwards, saying things like, 'I'd like to unwrap Tim Healy in my Valentine package.'

But now I find that I'm watching women looking at Matthew. It makes me feel proud and I'm very aware of my friends thinking, 'How old will he be in another ten years?' That's slightly disconcerting – and it's even worse when they start trying to work out how old Louis is going to be in ten years' time!

Does he know the little things about you?

KATE: According to a recent *Daily Mail* survey of 2,000 men, 6 out of 10 blokes don't know their women as well as she might like. The little things tripped them up: 12 percent of the men polled didn't know their partner's eye colour; 10 per cent didn't know her date of birth; a whopping 30 per cent didn't have a clue about her bra size. I'm not surprised about that!

COLEEN: How can you not know about them?

KATE: All Ray needs to know is that they are big.

COLEEN: He would just make hand gestures to a shop assistant!

KATE: So can we really expect our men to know the little things about us?

COLEEN: No! Not a chance in hell.

KATE: Does Ray know the colour of your eyes?

COLEEN: He knows the colour of my eyes and he knows my date of birth. That's it. Something did really shock me recently when my sister was there and we were talking about horoscopes. I said, 'Do you know what sign I am, Ray?' He didn't have a clue! I know that's like, so what? in the grand scheme of things, but I was so annoyed. 'We've been together ten years and you don't know that I'm a Pisces!' I said.

LESLEY: *We* all knew.

JANE: Did you dump him for that?

KATE: Do you read his stars?

COLEEN: Yes.

KATE: Stop! He doesn't deserve it.

JANE: It isn't worth it Col.

COLEEN: I have to say that we once played a Mr and Mrs type of game and we came last. We were so rubbish! The only subject we got every question right about each other was sex.

LESLEY: That's the really important stuff.

COLEEN: Oh, it's so not!

LESLEY: I think all this other stuff is a bit trivial really. I don't think Peter would know my eye colour unless I was stood in front of him with my eyes open at the time. Men don't know these little things, but I can't say that I'm all that bothered. I think all that's a bit girly. I'd much rather he knew the answers to the big things, like what we expect out of life, or what we want our kids to be doing. In the limited time I have to talk to him, I'd rather talk to him about that.

COLEEN: Boring that. I don't know his horoscope, but I don't care what he wants to do with his life.

KATE: And let's face it, Lesley, your bra size is a big thing!

LESLEY: Well, there you go, you see.

COLEEN: No wonder you are on *Loose Women*, Lesley.

LESLEY: To keep you company, love.

JANE: I have to say that Ed doesn't know my date of birth, mainly because I haven't told him what it is. I don't want him to know how old I am.

COLEEN: He probably thinks you're 25.

JANE: He thinks I'm in my thirties and I want to stick to that, really. I just sort of gloss over it every now and again. He does know my eye colour, but I don't think he knows all the other things. I'm not right fussed about it.

COLEEN: Ray has no idea of my natural hair colour. Mind you, neither have I, now.

JANE: It's grey.

KATE: Men just don't function with the same level of detail that we do. One of Darren's best friends, in fact his oldest friend in the world, has just spilt up with his girlfriend. Not so long ago, he came over to our house before the two of them went off together on a three-hour car journey and I said, 'How's your girlfriend?' 'We've split up,' he said. He obviously didn't want to talk to me about it, so I thought, it's OK, I'll get all the details from Darren at breakfast tomorrow. So in the morning, I said, 'So what happened? Is it alright?' 'I don't know,' Darren said. 'He doesn't want to talk about it.' Three hours in a car: what else do you talk about?

COLEEN: The worst is when your husband rings up about a friend who has had a baby.
　　'What was it?' you ask.
　　'Well, a baby.'
　　'What did it weigh?'
　　'I don't know! I wasn't there.'

How long does it take to get to know a man really well?

LISA: Years! You can think you know someone but when something momentous happens, like a bereavement or a lifestyle change, they can surprise you. So many things happen in relationships that are sent to try you.

I remember when Paul's sister Lynne passed away. It was a really difficult time for him and his mum and family. As his partner, it was a difficult time for me, because I didn't have the tools to deal with that sort of stuff, although I didn't realise that until it actually happened. You think you know somebody and you think you're giving them what they need, but actually you can find out that you're not even close to it. So you're being naive if you think that you truly know somebody, because then something will happen that will make them react in a way that you don't recognise.

Relationships are partly about growing and adapting to each other's changes. You roll with the waves and you take them and you come, learning as you go. But I don't think you ever truly get to know somebody.

LYNDA: It takes forever to get to know a man. You can pass Mr and Mrs quiz shows and know all about people's food preferences and habits without actually knowing anything very deep about them.

I don't know whether I'm stupid, selfish or self-obsessed, but I just don't work like that. On our most recent wedding anniversary, we went to Venice. I thought to myself, since we're in Venice, I don't need to get a card. Well, of course, he had bought me a beautiful card and presented it to me. I said, 'Let's get this straight now. How long have we known each other?'

'Six years.'

'So you know that I don't do cards, but it doesn't mean to say I don't love you. You do cards, but you could be one of those men who buys flowers and then goes out shagging somebody else.'

'Yes, darling.'

I derive pleasure in learning about how somebody works, because I've never had that in a relationship before. I've always been so busy placating, calming, trying to make it better or keeping myself together that I've never before had this degree of comfort and calm. It gives you a chance to notice the other person!

One of the things I've learned with Michael is that if he gets really angry about something, instead of reacting immediately to his anger, becoming defensive or trying to calm him down, I can just let him be angry, knowing that it will soon dwindle. It feels so great not to be fighting someone all the time!

Betrayal is probably the most devastating thing that can happen in a relationship, because you torture yourself wondering, 'Why didn't I know? How could I not know?' The answer is that I think we all have degrees of denial within us, including the person who is deceiving you. He knows what he's doing is wrong and so will find a way of denying it to himself. How can you know what he's up to when he is blocking it out? It's very hard. How is it that women don't know when their husbands are serial killers or child abusers? Well, how would you know if he compartmentalises his behaviour and behaves totally normally with you?

I would never ever want to be quoted as saying, 'I know my partner inside out. I know him like the back of my hand.' I think that is courting disaster. There is always more to learn.

Michael has said that he would never be unfaithful and he could never forgive infidelity. He says you can never go back. I tend to agree with him. I don't think you can. Everything that happens after that is coloured by the infidelity, even a tiny thing like an incoming text on his phone. You're going to look at that phone and think, 'Who is that text from and what does it say?' when normally you wouldn't think twice about it.

I was in that kind of situation when I was married to my first husband; everything was a threat. I managed to live with it, but it was a kind of torture.

I would worry that if Michael was unfaithful to me and got away with it, the chances are he would do it again. Even if it was a one night stand and he was drunk and it didn't mean anything, it would always play on my mind. When he had to go away on a trip, I'd be thinking, 'Why wouldn't he have another one night stand?'

I honestly think you can avoid being unfaithful. I really, truly do. I have been in situations where I've been drunk, which is the only time I'd be likely to succumb, and a little voice has said, 'If you don't think you can handle it, just walk away. Don't go to the hotel room and see how far things go. Go home!'

Could you cope with infidelity in your life?

ZOE: Absolutely not. I've said this so many times. Then people say, 'Couldn't you forgive him if it was, say, just once?' Maybe it's my insecurity, my weakness, because it takes strength to forgive that. I just can't. I wish I was strong, but for me it would just take the one time and then that would be it. I would never feel the same again.

I couldn't continue because the trust would be gone and then I'd be insecure about what he was doing. So it wouldn't be worth it for me. It really wouldn't. Even if I was still with my ex and Jake was involved, I just couldn't let it go and move forward. Whatever that makes me, it makes me. I just know from the heart that's the way it is for me.

SHERRIE: That is the problem. You wouldn't believe it was over, would you? Every now and then, the hurt would come up again. One glass of wine and it all comes back again. Then you start pointing the finger again. It doesn't go away.

I stayed for Keeley, even when I found out about the affair, but it was so wrong. It was wrong for her, because it was wrong for him and it was wrong for me. It destroyed us both. Had we both said, 'Look, this isn't working. Let's go our separate ways,' he'd have met somebody else and so would I. Maybe I'd have had more children and we would probably be OK about it all by now, perhaps even on speaking terms.

JANE: Any divorced couple will know that their kids want mummy and daddy to be together, no matter what. I'm not going to sit here and judge anybody for any infidelity, because you just don't know the story behind it. I know I keep harping back to the old days, but you just used to turn a blind eye. You had a certain respect for the person you were with, because actually sex is a very small part of a relationship. If you bring three kids into the world, it's difficult for a woman just to up and go. OK, women are a lot more financially secure now, but even so. And in my mother's day, that would never have happened, because women couldn't fend for themselves.

ZOE: That's why they didn't leave.

JANE: I've known a lot of couples who have had indiscretions, but there has been more to the relationship than the sex side of it. It all depends on sexual chemistry. Some people go off it very easily. Some people have a higher sex drive. I don't think sex is the be-all and end-all.

SHERRIE: I agree with that, but that's not the point. It's the lies, secrets and deceit. You lose respect for that person then, because you realise that you have been with somebody who has told you lies for years. They're not the person you thought you married.

ZOE: Absolutely, but the point you are making, Jane, is that it was just sex and sex is only a part of the relationship. I disagree, because I think that somebody holding you and touching you is a big part of a relationship. To think that they have done that with somebody else is difficult. It is for me, anyway. It's not the sex so much as the affectionate side, the loving side.

JANE: No but there is a different side to sex. There are the first two, three or five years of sex and then there's that wonderful relationship that comes afterwards.

SHERRIE: Or doesn't.

JANE: Or doesn't. I think it's a personal thing. If you can put up with it and still want the happy life and the house and everything you have worked for, then maybe you should go out and have a fling yourself. Maybe do it that way. I know I've got a different attitude to you. It's just that I've seen so many people who have had a wonderful family life and, just because the sex side wasn't right, it didn't mean to say they had to lose that.

SHERRIE: But there are certain people who shouldn't be married. Maybe they should always be single. As a married person, I would want fidelity and for that person to be there for me. Isn't trust the basis of marriage?

JANE: It takes two people to make a marriage work. If you are that negative about it, then get out of it.

Why does sexual infidelity matter so much?

LYNDA: Sexual infidelity matters because it is so intense. Even if the person being unfaithful is pissed, for that brief moment he or she is focused on the object of their passion at the height of passion. The thought of the person you love being in that heightened moment of passion with somebody else is unbearable. Of course, if you love somebody very much, you may be able to say to them, 'It is unbearable but I love you and I will try and live with it.' But it will be hard.

Some of us know people who say, 'I don't fancy my husband anymore. I love him, but I don't fancy him, and I've got to get sex somewhere.' To that I say, no, don't stay in the marriage. I'm sorry, but there is no instance where you have to be unfaithful to your partner. The fact that you don't fancy your husband and manage to find ways of not making love to him doesn't make it all right for you to shag somebody else. You should sit down with him and say, 'I don't fancy you anymore. If we have to live apart because of that, it's better to do that than lie.'

I have talked about all of this with Michael. 'What would you do if a woman came to your room?' I once asked.

'I'd get out of the room,' he said. 'I'd put distance between us.'

Some people say that thinking it is as bad as doing it. No, it's not! You can't help thinking these things and you should be sensible enough to recognise it as temptation. It's so selfish to indulge it.

Can you cope with sexual rejection?

ANDREA: When former *Corrie* star Tina O'Brien broke up from co-star Ryan Thomas, he reportedly said to her, 'You don't do it for me anymore.' It begs the question, can a relationship survive if one partner physically rejects the other?

LYNDA: Well, as you know I had an unconsummated marriage with my first husband. I won't go into the detail of why I married somebody that didn't fancy me, but basically he could make love to someone if it was a one-night stand, if it was grubby sex, but he couldn't make love to the woman he loved. Apparently, it's quite common. It was devastating and had a devastating effect on me. To lie next to someone who doesn't want to touch you, night after night, is awful.

CAROL: How long did you put up with that?

LYNDA: A year. I knew that there was a problem, but like all women who live in hope that we can change our men, I thought it would get better if I gave him enough love. A relationship can break down for all sorts of reasons, but if the sex isn't right, it is terribly noticeable. Still, I see no reason ever to turn round to somebody and say, 'I don't fancy you, because you're ugly,' or 'because you don't turn me on.' You can just say, 'That's the end.' You don't have to be personal about it.

CAROL: Did that affect your future choices, then?

LYNDA: It did, yes. I've always said that I think passion and a sexual relationship is incredibly important. It's not that it holds the relationship together, but if it's not there, or it's wrong, you become very aware of it. When it's right and it's fine, you don't think about it.

CAROL: But the question is, can you get past that? Can you be in a relationship where someone might reject you for a while – or you might reject them for a while – and then get back to it?

LYNDA: Yes, but that's different.

ANDREA: That's the normal ebb and flow of a relationship.

CAROL: I think some people can't. At the moment, I don't know what it's like to be rejected in this relationship, because I never have to ask.

ANDREA: Yes, but it's still very new. Your relationship is only two years old.

CAROL: Exactly, that's what I'm saying. I can't imagine what it would be like to sleep in the same bed as someone night after night and not have that physical contact, because it is a huge part of it. If it happened regularly and I thought something was wrong, I don't think I could live with it.

LISA: I have lived with it. Like you say, it's the ebb and flow of a normal relationship and there are times when you're physically connected and other times when you're not so physically connected. I don't think that those times necessarily mean the end of the relationship. It could be a number of things: you could have a new baby; it could be hormones; or it could be a medical condition, like a thyroid problem that you're not aware of.

I can understand how that part of a relationship is very, very important and can be essential, but it's not just about finding someone physically attractive. A relationship can go a lot deeper than that. I don't think it should be over just because the physical side has waned.

To say to somebody, 'I don't find you physically attractive,' is just so incredibly unnecessarily hurtful. I can't imagine how painful it must be to be with a man who doesn't want to have sex with you on a long-term basis, because in my experience, every man I've met wants it all the time! And I'm not blowing my own trumpet by saying that.

ANDREA: But that makes it doubly hurtful, because there's part of you that must think, well, men want it all the time, so if he doesn't want it with me, I must be the worst person on the planet. It's a huge rejection, especially if you've just had a small child, because your hormones have changed. I think this is more common than people realise amongst couples who have just had children, especially after the first child, because the men go from being centre of attention to finding that suddenly the woman doesn't have as much time for them anymore. A lot of men can't necessarily cope with that.

CAROL: But if you're talking about the end of a relationship, sometimes one of you knows it's been over for a long time, much longer, maybe, than the other person is willing to accept. So in those cases, maybe it's important to say something that is so honest and so hurtful that the person can move on and can accept that the relationship is over.

LISA: That's wrong.

CAROL: I'm not talking about a marriage necessarily or when you've just had a baby or anything like that; I'm talking about ending a relationship. Sometimes you need to say the words that someone doesn't want to hear.

LYNDA: Don't you think, 'I don't love you anymore,' is enough? You don't have to say, 'You're ugly. I don't fancy you.'

CAROL: Haven't you been in a relationship before where you've said that and people just think, oh, they don't know what they're saying. Then you carry on with it and carry on with it – I've done it! I've stayed in a relationship for much longer than I should have done, knowing someone didn't love me.

LISA: Just because you're angry and it's the first thing that comes into your head, you cannot end a relationship by saying something that's spiteful and nasty. You have to be truthful when you end a relationship and, if you're going to leave somebody heartbroken, don't make them feel like they've got absolutely no self-esteem and self-worth as well at the end of it.

CAROL: That's what I'm saying: sometimes you have to be totally truthful and say what somebody doesn't want to hear, in order for them to be able to move on and know that it's definitely over.

LISA: Would you leave someone because they've become physically undesirable?

CAROL: Look, I don't find anybody physically undesirable!

LYNDA: Carol, I don't fancy you anymore!

CAROL: Argh! It's over, Bellers, it's over! Move on!

When Kathryn Bigelow beat her ex-husband James Cameron to the Oscar for Best Director, the press dubbed it 'the sweetest revenge on the ex'. So can you ever be really be happy when life goes well for an ex?

LISA: No, not that well! He's sat there at the Oscars; both your names are called out; and your ex-wife gets to go up! Obviously, it depends how you break-up, but you just kind of want your ex to go away, don't you? But if she wins an Oscar, she's everywhere. She's on the telly, in the papers and in magazines. You just don't want to faced with that all the time.

ANDREA: Especially if you were both up for the same prize.

LISA: I think if you are in the same profession, it's a really hard pill to swallow. I wouldn't do very well with that, at all.

DENISE: Does it depend on how you split up with a person? With a few of the exes that I've had I would have to kill myself if they did well, because they wouldn't deserve it. A couple of exes in particular wouldn't deserve that type of success and they would be coming over as a nice person and I'd want to tell the world they were horrible.

ANDREA: But that's just according to you, because of your experience with them. They might deserve it.

DENISE: No, they are just horrible, Andrea; they just are horrible. But there are a couple of exes with whom I broke up really amicably and I would be thrilled if they were successful. Well, it depends how you define success. It's not necessarily winning Oscars. But I'm thrilled that this particular ex of mine is now happily married with a child and doing well in his chosen career.

LISA: I think it's quite difficult for your current partner if you've got an ex and everyone keeps saying, 'Did you hear? They just won an Oscar!' Or if they're saying to you, 'I can't believe how successful they are. They were rubbish when they were with you, but look at them now!'

It would make you want to shout at your ex, 'Go away! Take your Oscar and go and live somewhere else.'

ANDREA: My ex and I have been apart for five or six years now. He makes documentary films and I would genuinely be hand on heart pleased for him and proud of him if he did well, because I always knew he had it in him.

I wonder if there are people saying, 'Look how well he is doing now without her. She obviously held him back.' I don't know; maybe the chemistry didn't work for us. Maybe I propped him up too much or pushed him. Now I'm really genuinely pleased that he is doing well.

LISA: He could give you a job in one of his documentaries!

SHERRIE: I don't want to come across as a bitter person here . . .

ANDREA: I sense a 'but' . . .

SHERRIE: . . . but when somebody says, 'I saw your ex the other day. He looks great. He looks so much happier now!' I'd love to be very generous and say, 'It's fantastic. I'm just so thrilled.' But suddenly that hate comes in and you lose that generosity completely, don't you?

ANDREA: The bile rises!

SHERRIE: There's somebody in 'my business' that I was with once – and he has done very well and did win things. I honestly genuinely tried to sit there and cheer him on, but instead it came out, 'Eurgh!' even though I don't want to be like that.

ANDREA: What about outside of work life? If one of your ex-partners moves on and you can see that they're happily married with somebody else. Are you happy for them, then?

SHERRIE: It's still hard, isn't it? Of course, I'm talking about a bad break-up, not a really nice amicable break-up, where you are now friends. If it's a bad break-up, you are looking at somebody that you had a bad time with, who is now happy, but you're on my own, so it feels even worse. Also, if you have a child, you think, what if they have a child who will then interact with my child? I think it is really hard to be that generous. If I'm truthful, I can't be.

ANDREA: Could you do it, Lisa?

LISA: I think when kids are involved, it's really complicated.

SHERRIE: It is.

LISA: I think it is a totally different thing then, but if there are no kids involved and he is with another woman who is younger, prettier and he is happier with her, then I would hate it!

How do you cope when women pay lots of attention to your man?

KATE: Darren is a DJ and I've seen these women in action. In the early days I used to go along to a lot more of his gigs and there would be dancers literally in gold bikinis, if you were lucky! They'd be giving it a bit of that and a bit of this – in a bikini! You have to be a bit secure about yourself to be able to deal with that. To be honest, I thought it was quite funny. I thought, well at least I don't have to go to work in a bikini. I've got something going for me!

LYNDA: I have to tell you, Mr Spain would love that. He would be thrilled. But he now has a kind of infamy about him, partly because of the nickname I've given him. When I'm doing *Calendar Girls* on tour, I come out to talk to all these lovely ladies at the stage door and they rush past me to talk to him! I'm like, 'Oh, hello?'

But that is the nature of the beast. If you're the other half of an MP or anybody in the public eye, you have to take it

Duncan was finding it hard to keep his eye on his Mr. Whippy...

with a pinch of salt and hope and assume that it is meat and veg to them. They see it all the time. Meat and veg! If you're a young woman and you don't want your other half to talk to the opposite sex, then you have to sort your head out.

COLEEN: It's a terrible insecurity on your part if you can't handle it at all. I mean, Ray is such a flirt, but he is so open about it. We just laugh about it. When he sees you, Kate, it's 'you know you want me, Kate. Just deal with it.' He does that to women. He says, 'You want me, don't you?'

'No, seriously, you can have him,' I say. 'Don't worry about me.'

KATE: It's a bit of a double hander between the two of you, isn't it? It's a little skit. Because you know there is no intention behind it.

COLEEN: There is no intention behind it and we know where the line is. It's OK to flirt if you are openly flirting and having a laugh about it. But it's different when they go beyond that line. If Ray is having a laugh and doing all his Rayisms, as we call them, then that's fine. But if all of a sudden I looked across the room and he was quietly talking to someone and had been talking to that one person for 20 minutes, then I would be really annoyed. That's a different kind of flirting.

Does it seem fair that men can father children into their eighties, but women can't? Is it a step forward for women to be having kids in their fifties and sixties?

COLEEN: I think we've become very selfish. It's all about what we want. We don't have children because we want our career, so we put off having them and then all of a sudden we think we're missing out and we do want kids, so we'll have them now, however we can! I also found out recently that there's been a massive rise in breast cancer because women are waiting so long to have children.

The problem is that you don't really think about the kid. It's different if you've been trying for years and been unsuccessful after going down the IVF route and all of that. I have a friend who was trying from the age of thirty-eight and didn't have a baby until she was forty-nine – that's different. But the idea of a woman who all of a sudden at fifty decides that she's had enough of her career and wants children doesn't quite sit with me, even though I'm sure she would be a fabulous parent.

Mind you, it's really easy for me to say it, because I have three beautiful kids. I always wanted children, even when I was at school. Had I not been able to have them, I would have gone through hell and high water to have them, whatever procedures there were. I'm not against IVF, but there has to be a cut-off point, when you either adopt, because there are so many kids out there who aren't wanted, or you accept that you missed your chance.

And kids can be cruel. Ciara said to me recently, 'Do you know, you're the oldest mum in my class?' I said, 'Cheers,

Ciara!' I think she's right, too – I am the oldest mum in her class.

Up until last year, Ray and I talked about having another one. I panicked, knowing that soon the decision won't be my decision, but Mother Nature's decision. I was thinking, should I get another one out before that happens?

Ray said, 'If we had one now, by the time it's ten, I'd be sixty-two and they'll be saying, "Your granddad's here to pick you up."'

'You don't look fifty-two and you certainly don't act it,' I said.

'No, but I will be. That's the point.'

I did understand what he meant – there is such a thing as being too old, for men as well as women. In the end, I thought, well, I have had three and it is tiring and hard on your body . . .

DENISE: It's difficult, because you have to take each case separately. I don't think it's fair on the children to be having babies at 66 years old, as some women are, just because by the law of averages, you are going to die in a few years. But at the same time I also know how powerful the biological urge to have children is, because of my own urge, even though it came when I was in my childbearing years.

The second time, I was in my forties, which some people would consider too old. But who are we to judge? I was on a TV show a year or so ago and there was a woman in the green room who'd had a baby at 58. She totally looked like the child's grandmother, but at the same time she was ecstatically happy and the child seemed ecstatically happy. So you just think, well, some people with young parents have a horrible life from the day they are born. At least this woman, even if she only sees the kid until it's 20, will have given her child a lot of love.

So I think each case has to be taken on its own merits really. However, I do wonder why men are genetically made to be able to keep fathering until they die.

COLEEN: So that they can die while their doing it? What a terrible thought!

Chapter 6

Bits and pieces

There are some topics that simply defy categorisation: men's wash bags, for a start. They tend to be in a league of their own! What about the clothes they choose to wear (unless we're talking uniforms, yum!)? Or even worse, the clothes they choose for you? How about their attitudes to money, health and free time?

Here's all the stuff we thought about after we'd dealt with the big issues like sex, relationships and, er, sex . . .

What do you see when you look in his wash bag?

COLEEN: I always look in it and think, God, I need to clean that out. He's got his shaving stuff in there, along with his deodorant and toothpaste, but he obviously doesn't put the lids on properly, because there are loads of bits of gunk in it. I wouldn't put my hand in it! I'd need a tetanus. Every Christmas I buy him a new one, so at least it's only a year's worth of gunk! His personal hygiene is very good though, thankfully. He's always very clean.

'Brenda, you do realise that we're only going away for one night?'

DENISE: Have I ever looked inside it? Not by choice. I have never gone upstairs and thought, 'I'll just take a little peek into his wash bag.' But obviously on the rare occasion when I pack if he is going away, then it's me that gets it together. What really does annoy me is that when he goes away, he always takes the family toothpaste with him, so when we go to clean our teeth that night, we have no toothpaste. He never says, 'I'm going to take the toothpaste,' and he never thinks to buy his own. It really annoys me, because it happens all the time. So sometimes after he's packed his case, I nip upstairs and take the toothpaste out, so that when he gets to his hotel, he won't have any.

He is a very minimal packer, which makes sense. I would never let him pack for a holiday or anything. I always do the packing for the family holiday. You know I would never trust him to do that properly. His excuse for taking hardly anything would be, 'Well, I will just buy it when I get there.' That's basically code for, 'I can't be arsed to look for things now.'

How do men survive without handbags? I mean how do they? Mine practically amputates my arm every day. People say, 'Let me hold your bag for you,' and when I hand it to them, their arm plummets to the ground. Thinking about it, I've got Tim's keys and his passport, along with my own and three of Louis's wrestler figures. Your husband or son is always saying, 'Can I just pop that in there?' Everybody seems to use a woman's handbag.

What about men and clothes?

COLEEN: I like Ray to make an effort if we're going out. It really does it for me when men smell nice, so I love it when he showers, puts on a clean shirt and some aftershave.

He buys his own clothes and sometimes, when we're shopping, he'll pick things out for me, saying, 'I love this. You should get it.' I take one look at it and think, oh dear! Or I think, he's got a completely different vision in his mind of what my body is! It'll be a little shoestring top that you can't wear a bra with and it wouldn't go round my knee, let alone my breasts. I think, that's how he wants me to be! He'll see it on the mannequin in the shop and say, 'That would look great on you.'

I'll say, 'Glue those two models together and stretch the top across them and that'll give you more of an idea of the way it will look!'

Sometimes, I'll see something like a patterned shirt and think, if I bought that, Ray would say it was hideous! Instead, he points to it and says, 'I love that!'

'What do you mean?' I say. 'It looks like something's vomited over it! How can you like that? I don't know you at all.'

He has hideous things in his wardrobe, because he's a hoarder. He has things from the Seventies and Eighties, including a Michael Jackson jacket with all the braiding. 'If you ever walk down the stairs in that jacket, we are getting divorced!'

'I'm telling you, it will be back in fashion one day,' he insists.

'Ray, you will never wear that again,' I say.

'How do you know that?'

'Because you're married to me! And I wouldn't be caught dead with you in that jacket, unless it's a fancy dress.'

DENISE: I don't like it when men are obsessed with designer stuff exclusively. I like them to look nice, but not to obsess about it or know too much about labels, unless they're my gay friends.

SHERRIE: I like clean and fresh men. I always love a man in a white, ironed shirt and tailored trousers or jeans. I love the smell of fresh, clean, crisp clothes, especially on a man, and I love a man in a suit. It's like a uniform, isn't it?

DENISE: And we know you love a uniform, Sherrie!

SHERRIE: Don't we all?

And men and shoes . . .

ZOE: I don't do men's feet. End of. I think they're horrible! Hairy toes. Yellow toenails. Don't get them out in flip-flops! It's not right. It's just wrong. I can't bear men's feet. I don't like to see them.

SHERRIE: They don't all have yellow toenails.

KATE: Who are you going out with, Zoe? You've been dating beasts, not men.

ZOE: You're not wrong! But no, I just don't like them. And don't get me started on men's summer shoes! What about those flip floppy things with just a strip across? Are they supposed to be trendy?

CAROL: The spongey ones with the bits round the top? Two straps you mean? Like sandals?

ZOE: Oh, I hate Jesus sandals, because you can see the hairy toes.

SHERRIE: What about the ones that are just like toes? Have you seen them? They look like hands walking. What is that all about?

CAROL: Men can look all right if they wear nice leather sandals, like criss-cross ones or flip-floppy style. But you're right: their feet do have to be nice. When I first met Mark, his feet were OK, but they weren't up to standard.

SHERRIE: So what did you do?

CAROL: I didn't make him do anything, but I did encourage him to go and have his toenails done. We were in Thailand at the time and everybody gets their toenails done in Thailand.

ZOE: I like to see a man with nice feet. Thailand, here I come!

SHERRIE: So when he had his nails done, what colour nail varnish did he have put on?

CAROL: No nail varnish! He just had them done and they looked nicer. But he has quite hairy toes, so I made him have his toes waxed. He thanks me for it because they do look nice now and he can wear sandals. He never used to wear sandals; he used to wear his trainers all the time on holiday. And he had this pair of trainers on in Thailand for two weeks! He never took them off. On the beach. Getting them wet. They were rank!

Eventually, we were in this hotel in Singapore and I came out of the bathroom and said to him, 'Oh for God's sake, put those trainers outside! They stink.'

'They are outside,' he said – and the door was shut! After that it was sandals.

KATE: I think the test of whether you really love someone or not is if you can bear their feet. I'm lucky that Darren has really nice feet. I do like his feet. He always looks nice in a flip-flop but he won't wear them because he can't do between-the-toes. Still, we have pedicures together on holiday, because I think it's a nice thing to do.

SHERRIE: You know the trouble with English men? Don't they always wear socks with their sandals? Why?

ZOE: To hide those hairy, yellow-toed feet!

SHERRIE: Then they have brown legs and these big white feet that stick out the end of them.

KATE: Ladies, you are hanging with the wrong guys!

On to men and money . . .

COLEEN: Ray is tight as anything. He's Victor Meldrew! He epitomises all those jokes about tight Yorkshire men, as I told him the other day. He's generous with his friends and family in terms of presents, but he literally counts the pennies the rest of the time.

Sometimes I'll have loose change in the pocket of my bag or coppers weighing down my purse, so I'll take them out and put them on the side. He goes mental! 'Ray, there's about twelve pence there,' I say in my defence.

'Yes, if you leave it there every day, all of a sudden it mounts up to £20!' he says.

'Shut up!' I say.

He obstinately puts it all in a bucket and when it's full, he takes it down to the change machine in the local supermarket. When I come home that day, he'll say, 'You know all those coppers you can't be bothered with? £97!'

Oh, I hate it when he's right!

SHERRIE: I know just what you mean, Coleen! I'm the same.

COLEEN: And the other day, we went to a toy superstore for Ciara's birthday and Ray was outraged that the car park was Pay and Display. 'You mean that we're going to spend a fortune in there and they're making us pay for the parking?'

'It's only fifty pence for two hours,' I said.

'That's not the point though, is it? It's still 50p.'

He grumbled all the way around the shop. 'It's only 50p!' I kept saying. 'I can understand you complaining if it's a fiver.'

'It doesn't make any difference how much it is. It really annoys me.'

'Victor, just put the money in!'

Having said that, because he's like that with money, for the first time in my life I actually have money. Because otherwise, I'm a bugger with it.

SHERRIE: But you're not a spendthrift, are you?

COLEEN: Well, I don't come home having bought Jimmy Choo shoes or anything; I can't think of anything worse. I'm my mother's daughter in that way. I'm shocked when someone says, 'They were a bargain; they were only £800.' For a pair of shoes? For that much money, I'd want the coat, the hat, the bag, the shoes and the holiday! But I'm always spending money on my family or the house, so it's great that Ray reins me in.

Since I've met him, I've never worried about tax bills, because he's always put my tax away. So that's brilliant.

LISA: My grandfather was very careful with money. He wrote down the money he lent people in a book and he charged interest on it. He wouldn't lend any to my nan, because he thought she'd go down the bingo hall, so she used to pretend that she was borrowing it for a colleague. 'I'll drop it off to him,' she'd say, pocketing it. Then she'd have to pay him back with interest!

Do men in uniform do it for you?

SHERRIE: I love polo players! Well, it's a kind of uniform, because they have those big leather boots up their thighs and very nice tight white trousers. Oh yes! I like a naval officer, too; Richard Gere is quite sweet in *An Officer and a Gentleman*, isn't he? And I like the American GIs in their khaki and all that, with the leather belt; and RAF, I like a bit of blue. I do like uniforms. But what about a man in black tie, evening dress? Don't you think that is gorgeous?

JANE: I did go for a man in uniform once and I ended up marrying him – but it's a bit of a shock when he turns up with his flip-flops and shorts on. That's a bit of a comedown.

SHERRIE: Is the charisma gone then?

JANE: Yes, sometimes it all goes with the uniform. You are lucky if you get somebody who looks good in both. Don't just fall for the uniform!

SHERRIE: Because it lies on the bed without a body!

JANE: That's it.

LISA: I like a man in suit. I think suits are flattering to most bodies. And if they've got a suit, you know they've got a job – unless they're going to court!

ANDREA: What kind of look do you go for?

JANE: I do like a man in a suit.

ANDREA: You see, I'm the odd one out here. I like a nice clean T shirt, a nice pair of jeans, a nice pair of boots and a man smelling all lemony and clean, like he's just got out of the shower. A little bit of lemony aftershave.

LISA: A big old belly in a T shirt.

ANDREA: Well, I never really think about the belly side of things! That's just the look I like. Quite casual, jeans and a T shirt and clean.

JANE: What is it with you and cleanliness?

SHERRIE: You don't like it dirty, do you?

ANDREA: Well!

SHERRIE: Oh, excuse me, sorry.

JANE: Not that type of dirty, anyway!

Should you try and take control of your relationships destiny and pin down your man?

ZOE: Well, I've pinned down a few men in my time!

CAROL: What properly, though? I mean, are you always in control? Do you have to be in control?

ZOE: I know what you mean! Well, when I was 20, I had a relationship with a guy who was quite a bit older than me and he controlled everything about my life. Everything. When I managed to walk away – actually, run away – from that relationship, I thought, I want to make decisions now. I think I'm still at that stage.

I'm a little bit bossy. When I got married, although my ex-husband proposed and everything, I said, 'Right, yes, I will marry you and let's do it next month. We'll go to Las Vegas.' I organised it!

I suppose I do push things along a little bit and maybe you shouldn't do that. I don't know. Maybe it's better to take it easy.

KATE: Especially with a big thing like a wedding.

SHERRIE: Yes, you should stop being pushy.

ZOE: Men like it, don't they?

KATE: No, they don't like it.

SHERRIE: I did it, Zoe; I organised everything at my wedding. His suit, his underpants, his socks, his shoes . . . I booked the church and the reception in the vicar's garden next to the church. But what I forgot to say to the vicar's wife was, 'Could you take your washing off the line?' So all the pictures are of me with the vicar's knickers in the background!

Back to the point, men don't like being pushed and organised.

CAROL: They go along with it, because they are kind of lazy and would rather somebody else organised it all. But it's not a good idea.

KATE: You don't want to marry someone because they are too lazy not to go along with it.

CAROL: I'm not saying it's a good idea. I think it's a shocking idea. Like Zoe, we have all been in controlling relationships. You only have one, though. You don't let it happen again. Either it makes you into a bit of a control freak yourself or you learn from it and make sure you don't do it.

I have to check myself sometimes when I am talking about my wedding – see I'm doing it again! Because it's not my wedding, it's *our* wedding. Mark can be sitting right there and I'll be saying, 'I don't really want to get married there. I think I'm going to get married . . .' It's me, my, me, my, me, my. It's not 'our' or 'we'. I always realise I'm doing it and I stop it.

But if you have been in the situation where you have been dictated to, you can't help it. I completely organised my first marriage, but he dictated when it was going to be and it had to be on a certain date. You don't let that happen again.

SHERRIE: Little Mark goes up to his room and shuts the door and reads his little books and says, 'When will you stop shouting at me?' Doesn't he?

CAROL: No, he doesn't. He goes up and looks at his little diary and says, 'Oh, I don't think I can. I've got to go to school that day.'

KATE: When we got engaged, I had never dropped a hint to Darren that I wanted to get married. It came completely out of the blue, which made it all the more special, because I knew it was something he really wanted to do. He had been married before, so it was certainly something I was never going to pressure him into.

We decided, OK, we are going to get married and we're going to go away to do it, to try and contain it, because I come from quite a big family. Oh, but it all got horribly out of hand! In the long term, he actually played a very good game with me, because he went along with it. So I'm dragging him around Tuscany. Why Tuscany? We had never been there, but we decided that, yes, Tuscany would be great. We went to Tuscany looking for a small boutique wedding and we came back having booked a medieval hamlet. That's a village! For 250 people! I spent about three weeks phoning people and saying, 'Right, it's going to be Italy.'

We set the date and I was literally writing the cheque for the venue when I thought, I feel pregnant! Like how would I know? I'd never been pregnant before in my life. But I did a pregnancy test and I was pregnant! So we called the wedding off, because Ben was due within six weeks of the wedding and I thought, now, that's a bad idea.

Now a big wedding just seems vulgar and flash and a terrible waste of money. If we do it, we will do it his way which means small, low key, cheap and . . .

CAROL: You're dictating how you'll do it his way!

KATE: What he wanted all along was a small wedding, but he indulged me and went along with it and now I give him what he wants.

SHERRIE: So he actually manipulated you.

ZOE: When my ex said, 'Let's get married,' I said, 'OK, we will get married in Vegas, because if I don't marry you straight-away, I will never marry you.' Married in Vegas; divorced in Colchester!

What do you reckon to a recent survey that says that a man has more time on his hands than a woman does?

DENISE: I don't think they needed a survey to work that out.

ANDREA: Would our lives be easier if men had more time to themselves or less?

LISA: I would like it if Paul had more time off, because he really does work hard. He has a factory in China, so he has to be up at all hours of the night and it can be quite difficult for us to find a moment to be together. So when he does have free time, I like to be with him and if he has free time and he doesn't spend it with me, I get really miffed.

ANDREA: Do you?

LISA: Yes I do, a bit. I like 'we' time.

DENISE: So what kind of thing would he be doing if it wasn't with you?

LISA: Er, fishing.

DENISE: But you go fishing with him.

LISA: I know.

DENISE: You are like a perfect Stepford wife.

LISA: Yes, I love fishing. I'm very good at fishing. I caught a fish once.

ANDREA: But does he like you going with him, or is it a case of, 'Cooey, guess what?'

LISA: Yes it's a bit like that. 'Wahay!' Beau and I go with him. We didn't have a lot of 'we' time when I was working really hard, so I cherish it. I really crave it.

DENISE: I don't want Tim to have any more 'me' time than he has already. He gets enough free time to do things. He's always saying that he's going to Sainsbury's, when he's really going to the pub. Even Matthew says, 'Why does Dad keep saying that he's at the supermarket, when he is actually at the pub?' He just leaves his car in the pub car park. It's so obvious!

I don't like to generalise, but I will when I say that men don't feel guilty about 'me' time. They don't give it a second thought! Even the most lovely men I know. Whereas women are more likely to sacrifice our 'me' time.

I know I feel guilty if I go for a massage, which I think we are all quite entitled to, because we all work a lot in this day and age. Yet I'll say to people, 'I'm just at the physiotherapist.' Why do I say that? Because I feel guilty about saying I'm having a massage!

SHERRIE: But you don't like Tim having any time! You don't even like him going out on his bike.

DENISE: I do. You're thinking of one particular argument over his bike. That was selfish. Because, Sherrie, I'd asked him to do things for me and he said he had to go out on his motorbike. Why do you have to go out on your motorbike for an hour? You don't have to!

LISA: He wanted to get away from you!

DENISE: The other thing that gets my goat is golf. It is the most selfish sport in the entire world, where the etiquette says that you can't have your mobile phone on. Now I get that, but there is no law that says you can't check your phone to see if your wife might have rung you!

SHERRIE: The thing is, you have your golf widows, and then there's the gym, the tennis and the fishing. They've always got something to do, haven't they? I always remember my ex saying, 'I'm just taking the car out for a drive.' He was gone for five hours!

DENISE: Well, that is the same as the bike law, obviously.

SHERRIE: What was he actually doing, though? I didn't know where he had really gone. Also, men are slower than women, aren't they? They take longer doing everything. They're on a slower time frame than women. We rush about, doing whatever we do, using up whatever 'me' time we have. But when I have 'me' time and I'm having a massage, one hand will be holding the phone while I'm talking to somebody, another hand will be turning a page and I'll be doing the shopping in my head . . .

ANDREA: You see, I disagree. You say men are slow, but I think it is the other way around. Women are very good at pootling. We fill our time with lots and lots of things to do. 'I'll just do a bit of this and I'll just do a bit of that.' Whereas men do one thing at a time.

LISA: Because sometimes they can only manage one thing at a time.

ANDREA: Yes, and they do one thing and then they think, right I've done that. I'm going to stop and have a rest. But actually, who has got it right? I think they've got it right, because we fiddle about so much and so we don't have as much 'me' time.

DENISE: I think there is something called 'working mother's guilt', so we almost feel like we have to be doing something for the children, all the time.

LISA: Yes, and you are right about the massage thing. I've thought, I won't go out and have a massage. I will try and get one in the house. And I'm on the floor in my bedroom and I can hear Beau at the door, saying, 'Mum, Mum!'

SHERRIE: What do you do in your 'me' time, anyway? I've lost the art of what to do with me on my own.

ANDREA: Walk the dog. I really enjoy walking the dog, because then I feel like I'm multitasking. The dog needs walking, so I'll walk it. But I'm also having a lovely walk on my own.

LISA: You're not. You've got the dog with you.

SHERRIE: We are talking about 'me' time, Andrea. You've got to do something for yourself. Get in the house, take all your clothes off and just be there on your own. What about that?

LISA: Sometimes you can have more stimulating conversations with the dog.

ANDREA: Yes that's why I like walking the dog!

What's your man like at sewing?

KATE: According to a new survey, men find it more difficult to darn a hole than to cook a roast dinner. The survey also revealed that two-fifths of men said that would have trouble sewing up a hole in a jumper, while a fifth of men admitted that they would struggle to cook a roast dinner. So should a man be able to stitch and darn and take care of his own business?

COLEEN: Normally, this is where I would go off on one about my Ray and how useless he is. But I'm going to have a day off from that, because I have to say that he's brilliant at sewing, whereas I can't sew a button on. If a little button falls off Ciara's school summer dress, I'll say, 'I'm just off to the shop, love, to get a new dress.' Because they're only about £1.99! But he says, 'No, we'll just sew the button back on.'

Being the youngest of a very large family, I just never had to do it. I had five older sisters, two brothers and my mum was brilliant at all of that. So I never had to and no one ever bothered to say, 'Well, you should, whether you have to or not.' Whereas Ray is brilliant at it.

KATE: Well done, Ray!

COLEEN: This is the first topic we've discussed in ten years where I've been able to say he's good! Credit where credit's due!

KATE: I learned what little I know from my mum, because she was a whizz with the old Singer. In fact, everyone still drops

Janet had sent Brian to the beautician.
'You'll be fine dear. As you're always telling me, men have
a much higher pain threshold than women . . .'

their repairs round to my mum now. But I can darn and sew a little and I can put a hem on something. It's a basic of life, isn't it?

LYNDA: Only if you're taught it! Mr Spain is not a great sewer, but he can sew a button on and iron and he has the cleanest shoes in the whole world, because of being in the army. That's where they're taught. I know I bat on about this a lot, but it would be fantastic if they taught sewing and brought back Domestic Science in school, for both sexes. Then people would learn it as part of life's skills. It's all very well getting ten A star plusses, but when you've got no intention of going to university and the university doesn't want you anyway, you might just as well learn to sew a button on!

KATE: And pay a bill! Too right, Lynda; I think we should put you in charge of Education!

What about men and health?

LYNDA: My father was incredibly physical. He worked hard on the farm until his seventies, when he fell off the back of a truck while he was hedging. After an X-ray at Stoke Mandeville hospital, he was given the all-clear and sent home, when in fact he had broken a vertebra in his neck. He walked about for ten days before it was diagnosed, saying, 'I'm really in pain.' He could have died at any moment, but he was very low key about it.

LISA: What a hero! Men usually aren't very good at being ill, are they? Think of man flu! Having said that, I'm rubbish when Paul's ill.

'What's wrong?' I'll ask impatiently. 'Have you taken anything? Are you going to see the doctor?'

'No, I don't want to go and see the doctor.'

'Well, you're not going to get better then, are you?'

'I'm just saying I don't feel well.'

'Don't just tell me you're not well. Take something!'

'Why can't I just say I'm not well and then you say, '"You poor thing, what's wrong?"''

'But I asked you what's wrong and are you going to go to the doctor?'

'There's nothing a doctor can do.'

'What, are you a doctor now, then?'

'I'm not saying I'm a doctor.'

'Well, you're pretending you know better than the doctor.'

Then we'll have an argument, because he's ill! 'You can't be that ill, or you'd go to the doctor.'

SHERRIE: Men don't like going to the doctor. They won't talk about certain aspects of their health. They can be helped but it seems they don't want to be. It's so silly. My dad was like this with his prostate. He just wouldn't go to the doctor. 'It's all right, it's nothing,' he used to say.

'Dad, it might be something. You should go for a test,' I said. But he didn't listen. Maybe younger men are better about this kind of thing. I hope so.

LISA: No, they seem to think it's a waste of time. In the past, I've made appointments for Paul and made him go. I can see his point though, because he's gone in there with one thing and come out with about a million other things after having loads of tests. And once it's been decided that it's not whatever it was that they thought it was in the beginning, then they just send you home, because it's not what they thought it was. As long as it's not what they first thought it was, you'll be all right then, won't you?

Should we expect men to know what makes us tick?

So, finally, and to even things up a little, we thought it was only fair to ask . . .

SHERRIE: I sympathise when men say they don't understand what makes us tick. I think a woman is one of the most complicated creatures on this earth. Men are much simpler creatures. They tend to focus on one thing at a time, so if they are going to drive a car, they drive a car. If a woman is driving a car, she is thinking about the shopping and picking up the children, her shoes for the next day, bookings and jobs. All of that is going on while a woman is driving a car! Men do tasks one by one, whereas we do a thousand in one second. I think that's why we're so complicated. We complicate our lives and ourselves!

Conclusion

So there you have it, ladies: our take on fellas in all their, er, glory, from boys to men, teen idols to house husbands, first crushes and fantasy hunks to long-suffering other halves! We don't claim to have laid bare the inner man completely (although if we did he'd undoubtedly be wearing a pair of grubby psychic underpants) but we think we've come closer to understanding how the male brain works . . . Well, as close as we're likely to get!

But yes, it seems there really is something going on beneath those gradually balding scalps – whoops, we mean fine heads of hair – although it's still true to say that none of us can be absolutely sure what they talk about amongst themselves. We're fairly certain that it's sports and gadgets though, with the occasional outburst of appreciation for fit women and obvious areas of the female anatomy. Yawn: thank goodness they've got each other to talk to, because there are only so many George Clooney fantasies a girl can loop silently through her head without falling asleep!

What we do know is that we don't half love men, in spite of all their flaws, and we also recognise that sometimes they've got their hands full with us women. What's more, the way they fascinate and perplex us means that we'll never get bored of thinking and talking about them – and that's reason enough to celebrate the opposite sex, when we're not secretly contemplating bashing them over the head with the blooming remote!

We really hope you've enjoyed reading this book as much as we've enjoyed expressing our views and opinions in it. Hopefully it's given you pause for thought and more than a few belly laughs. Thank you so much for buying it. We never forget that we wouldn't be the Loose Women we are, without you.

Love the Loose Women xx